READING AND THE GIFTED CHILD

READING AND

THE GIFTED CHILD

A Guide for Teachers

By

DONALD C. CUSHENBERY, Ed.D.

Foundation Professor of Education
Director, Reading Clinic
University of Nebraska at Omaha
Omaha, Nebraska

and

HELEN HOWELL, Ed.D.

Professor of Education
University of Nebraska at Omaha
Omaha, Nebraska

CHARLES C THOMAS · PUBLISHER
Springfield · Illinois · U.S.A.

Published and Distributed Throughout the World by

CHARLES C THOMAS · PUBLISHER

Bannerstone House

301–327 East Lawrence Avenue, Springfield, Illinois, U.S.A.

© *1974, by* CHARLES C THOMAS · PUBLISHER

ISBN 0–398–03186–X

Library of Congress Catalog Card Number: 74–7043

With THOMAS BOOKS careful attention is given to all details of manu-
facturing and design. It is the Publisher's desire to present books that are
satisfactory as to their physical qualities and artistic possibilities and
appropriate for their particular use. THOMAS BOOKS will be true to
those laws of quality that assure a good name and good will.

Printed in the United States of America
K–8

Library of Congress Cataloging in Publication Data

Cushenbery, Donald C
    Reading and the gifted child.

    Includes bibliographies.
        1. Gifted children—Education—Reading. I. Howell, Helen, joint author.
II. Title.
LC3993.5.C87   371.9′53   74–7043
ISBN 0–398–03186–X

PREFACE

T HERE IS A noticeable lack of special educational programs for gifted children in the United States because many teachers entertain the philosophy that pupils of this type "can get it on their own." There exists a great need to dispel this feeling and to supply educators with pertinent, practical help for challenging the gifted and talented pupil. This volume has been designed to fulfill this objective.

All teaching suggestions which are described have been classroom-tested and found to be useful. Theory has been kept to a minimum and used for the sole purpose of providing background information. The manuscript was read by practicing educators to insure the usefulness of the material.

Appropriate references have been included at the close of each chapter for those readers who wish to pursue additional sources of information. The appendices contain a wealth of suggestions regarding the use of commercial materials. Since prices fluctuate considerably, this information has not been listed. Publishers' addresses have been included in a separate appendix.

ACKNOWLEDGMENTS

THE AUTHORS wish to acknowledge their indebtedness to the faculty and staff members of the Departments of Special Education and Elementary and Early Childhood Education of the University of Nebraska at Omaha for their constant encouragement while the manuscript was in the process of preparation.

We also wish to express our appreciation to Mrs. Jolene Medley, Miss Jean Zartner, and Mrs. Cheryl Estes for helping in the preparation of the appendices section and for aiding the authors in the pursuit of certain materials for the various chapters.

Our gratitude is extended to Mrs. Edwin K. Wright, the manuscript typist, for her patience and understanding. We are indebted to Mrs. Peggy Newkirk, the official proofreader, for her constructive criticisms with regard to format, content, and sentence construction.

Many classroom teachers and special educators supplied numerous suggestions with respect to teaching approaches and the use of various materials. Our thanks are extended to these outstanding educators of gifted children.

A volume of this magnitude consumed a large amount of time which has been subtracted from the hours which might have been spent with our families. We express our appreciation to the members of our families for their understanding attitude.

D. C. C.
H. H.

CONTENTS

READING AND THE GIFTED CHILD

CHAPTER I

UNDERSTANDING
THE GIFTED CHILD

O NE OF THE MOST challenging problems of classroom teachers
is that of providing an educational program for the child
who is below "normal" in the physical, emotional and/or intellectual areas. These difficulties make lesson planning a most difficult assignment and many teachers feel they have not had the
appropriate training for dealing with these kinds of pupils.

Pupils on the other end of the continuum, those who possess
such qualities as superior intelligence and intense curiosity,
present equally perplexing instructional problems for the teacher.
They complete regular classroom assignments in a brief period
of time and hope that their teacher will present them with challenges commensurate with their superior abilities. One of the
chief purposes for compiling this volume is to provide the classroom teacher and administrator with a compendium of practical
teaching suggestions and plans which can be employed with
these children.

In this chapter the following topics are explored: the identification of the gifted child, instructional needs and problems of
gifted children with regard to the teaching of reading and the
reading instruction goals for gifted children.

Identification of the Gifted Child

The identification of gifted children, in itself, appears to be a
debatable issue. There are those who feel that children identified
as gifted become objects of social scorn with jealousies developing among pupils not included in this special grouping. An additional argument against identification is described by Torrance: [1]

[1] Paul E. Torrance, *Gifted Children in the Classroom* (New York, The Macmillan Co., 1965), pp. 20–21.

3

Some teachers and laymen argue that it is useless to identify gifted-ness because "what is good for the average is good for all." This argument is simply not true. The results of practically every educational experiment that has taken into consideration different levels and kinds of ability provide an argument in favor of the importance of individualized instruction.

There are many reasons for identifying gifted children. These children need to be challenged and their exact academic competencies analyzed in order to plan a proper educational program. The Westside Community Schools (School District 66) of Omaha, Nebraska has developed an outstanding program of identification for gifted children.

The official school board policy indicates that district officials recognize that there are obvious individual differences between pupils and the system has an obligation to develop each pupil to his maximum potential level. A program for the gifted and talented has been developed for those pupils with high intelligence levels; outstanding leadership abilities, scientific capabilities, creativity, and artistic and musical talent; and those who have high potential but are underachievers.

One of the most difficult aspects of providing a proper educational program for the gifted child is that of identification. The word *gifted* has a variety of connotations. Some characteristics which have common agreement are those dealing with such items as general academic development, level of intelligence, degree of curiosity and leadership abilities.

A specific rating list which employs the use of numbers from 2 (low) to 4 (high) has been devised by Buhler and Guirl.[2] Their list consists of the following characteristics:

1. High academic achievement
2. Advanced vocabulary and reading level
3. Expressive fine arts talent
4. Wholesome personal-social adjustment
5. Early physical competence
6. Superior intellectual ability
7. Effectively work independently
8. Persistent curiosity

[2] Ernest O. Buhler, and Eugene N. Guirl, "The More Able Student: Described and Rated," *Vocational Guidance Quarterly* (Summer, 1960), pp. 217–221.

9. Strong creative and inventive power
10. Special scientific ability
11. High energy level
12. Demonstrated leadership abilities
13. Well-developed mechanical skills

This list of skills is representative of those frequently mentioned by various authorities on the gifted.

After determining the desirable characteristics which denote the gifted child, the next step should be to establish a program of identification with respect to these children. These procedures should be structured to fit into the pattern of the general testing program of the school and should be as comprehensive and functional as possible through the use of informal as well as formal devices. A large variety of tests should be used which sample a wide range of abilities.

An effective identification program should precisely delineate the interests of a gifted child, along with appropriate data regarding his academic achievement and overall personality, level of motivation, social status, motor skills and language abilities. This information should be used to provide an individualized program of instruction which will challenge the child to do his best work regardless of his racial, religious or socio-economic background. All pupils should receive the opportunity to participate in all aspects of the testing program, since truly gifted children are found in every type of school environment.

The Use of Standardized Tests in the Identification Process

While sole reliance should not be placed on the results of standardized tests, data from these instruments are used to a great degree in the identification of gifted children. Tests should be selected with careful consideration to their validity and reliability. (*The Mental Measurements Yearbooks* by Buros [Gryphon Press] contain critiques of many tests as well as information relating to validity and reliability.)

The most frequently used standardized tests for identification are the individual and group intelligence tests. Since definite attention can be given to each child, the use of individual measures such as the *Stanford-Binet* (Houghton Mifflin), *Wechsler*

Intelligence Scale for Children (Psychological) and *Wechsler Intelligence Scale for Adults* (Psychological) are preferred by many educators. Due to the immense amount of time required for mass testing, the exclusive use of individual tests is prohibitive. Because of this factor, many school authorities employ the use of group intelligence tests such as the *California Test of Mental Maturity* (California: McGraw-Hill); *Chicago Non-Verbal Examination* (Psychological); *Detroit Beginning First-Grade Intelligence Test* (Harcourt); *Kuhlmann-Finch Intelligence Tests* (Psychological); *Otis Quick Scoring Mental Ability Tests* (American Guidance); *Pintner General Ability Tests* (Harcourt); *SRA Primary Mental Maturity Test* (SRA) and the *Raven Progressive Matrices Test* (Psychological). The selection of a particular test should be based on the ages of the pupils to be tested, the training of the examiner and the use to be made of the test results.

Other standardized instruments such as the following are sometimes used for identification purposes:

Academic Promise Tests (Psychological) is a battery of separate tests for measuring verbal and numerical competencies.

California Test of Personality (California: McGraw-Hill) provides information relative to self and social adjustment.

Illinois Tests of Psycholinguistic Abilities (Illinois) consists of nine subtests designed to measure such aspects as verbal grammar and visual sequence.

Oseretsky Motor Proficiency Tests (American Guidance) lend valuable information relating to all major areas of motor proficiency.

Psychoeducational Profile of Basic Learning Abilities (Consulting) comprises a booklet for the summary of relative data regarding such aspects as language abilities, perceptual strengths, social-personal adaptivity and overall mental abilities.

Thematic Apperception Test (Psychological) is a projective personality instrument used by those clinicians with special training in its use.

Valett Developmental Survey of Basic Learning Abilities (Consulting) comprises over 200 learning situations in several areas including tactile discrimination, auditory discrimination, language development and visual discrimination.

Because of time, space, and personnel limitations, only a select number of tests would be administered in any given school situation. In many instances, tests would only be given in cases where there was legitimate doubt concerning the degree of giftedness present in a particular child. While many educators feel the preceding instruments should be used principally for diagnostic purposes, there is sufficient justification to use one or more for identification purposes as well. Many of the instruments demand a high level of competency on the part of the examiner with regard to test administration and interpretation; thus, unless such trained persons are available, use of the instruments should be restricted accordingly.

The results from achievement tests constitute an important way of measuring academic achievement in such areas as science, language arts, and mathematics. Gifted pupils are normally characterized by high scores on such tests, especially in vocabulary and general reading. A precise description of reading achievement tests can be found in Chapter VIII along with the addresses for ordering such instruments. At this point it is sufficient merely to point out some of the more commonly used achievement tests for identification and other purposes. These include the *California Achievement Tests* (California: McGraw-Hill); *Comprehensive Tests of Basic Skills* (California: McGraw-Hill); *Gates-MacGinitie Reading Tests* (Teachers College Press); *Iowa Every-Pupil Test of Basic Skills* (Houghton-Mifflin); *Iowa Tests of Educational Development* (Science Research Associates); *Metropolitan Achievement Tests* (Harcourt); *Sequential Tests of Educational Progress-STEP* (Educational Testing Service); *SRA Achievement Series* (SRA); *Stanford Reading Tests* (Harcourt); and *Wide Range Achievement Test* (Psychological). Since achievement tests evaluate many aspects of a child's academic ability, the scores from several instruments should be used before precise diagnostic decisions are finalized. The use of a given test should be determined after consulting the Buros volume and asking the opinions of local educational authorities who have administered the instrument in question.

The Role of Informal Instruments

Since the degree of reading interest is a criteria to be considered in determining giftedness, the use of commercial or informal reading inventories is recommended. The following reading interest inventory has been used by the author with a high degree of success.

READING INTEREST INVENTORY [3]

1. Name _____ Age _____ Grade _____
2. From what source(s) do you secure most of your free reading books?
   Friends _____ School Library _____ Community Library _____ Church Library _____
3. How many books have you borrowed during the past month? _____
   How many of the books did you read completely? _____
   Give the titles of some of the books. _____
   _____
4. Check the kinds of books which you like to read.
   Fiction _____ Mysteries _____ Sports_____
   Romance _____ Heroes _____ History _____
   Science _____
5. What kinds of hobbies do you have? _____
   _____
6. List the names of three television programs you like best.
   _____
7. Give a list of the states and countries which you have visited. _____
8. Mention the names of three of your favorite newspapers.
   _____

[3] From the book, *Reading Improvement in the Elementary School* by Donald C. Cushenbery. © 1969 by Parker Publishing Co., Inc., West Nyack, N. Y. and used with their permission.

9. Which of the following sections of the newspapers do you usually read?
   A. National and local news _____ D. Editorials _____
   B. Comics _____ E. Sports _____
   C. Feature stories _____ F. Other _____
10. If you had at least two hours a day to devote to free reading, what kinds of materials would you probably select? Why? __

_____

_____

_____

Responses from students who might fall in the gifted category will probably indicate:

1. Books read will be secured from two or more sources.
2. There will be evidence that a larger than average number of books have been read and that they have been read completely.
3. A wide variety of books on a number of subjects will be indicated.
4. Other pieces of information will support the idea that the respondent enjoys both functional and leisure time reading activities.

In addition to the screening devices and techniques described previously, some school authorities employ the use of informal teacher information forms for teacher recognition of those pupils who display exceptional creative potential.

The following screening and nomination form may be used by teachers for identifying gifted and talented pupils. Those students who are thus nominated should be given additional tests to make exact determinations.

SCREENING AND NOMINATION FORM FOR IDENTIFYING GIFTED AND TALENTED PUPILS

Pupil's Name _____ Teacher _____

Grade _____ Date _____ School_____

Check the column which best describes the pupil with regard to the function in question.

	Yes	*No*	*Sometimes*
1. Demonstrates ability to derive and employ a number of different approaches to finding a solution to a stated problem			
2. Displays capability of producing a large number of ideas for various situations.			
3. Uses many original procedures for solving problems and/or experiments which arise from everyday class assignments.			
4. Analyzes existing plans and policies and shows insights into possible alterations which may improve present situations.			
5. Remembers details and factual information and is able to transmit this data into main ideas and conclusions.			
6. Employs many mental images or concepts in response to any one of a variety of learning modalities which may be used by his teacher.			
7. Displays the ability to create an original story or play with an iden-			

	Yes	*No*	*Sometimes*

tifiable plot and climax which is believable and unique.

8. Shows that he can withhold judgment on a matter until he has had time to peruse all available facts.

9. Produces oral and written stories and poems which are written in a sequential manner.

10. Exhibits a knowledge of the meaning and use of a large variety of words and is able to place them in proper context.

11. Makes a story "come alive" by the use of vivid descriptions.

12. Demonstrates the ability to analyze the intentions and moods which are displayed by authors of novels and poems.

In this instrument, students with a large number of "yes" notations are given serious consideration for special programs for gifted and talented students.

Instructional Needs and Problems of Gifted Children with Regard to the Teaching of Reading

Until recent years, little research has been conducted concerning the need for any special program or provisions in reading for pupils considered gifted. During the 1930's some educators advanced the idea of teaching pupils to read at age four or younger; however, in light of the Morphett-Washburne study [4] which demonstrated that a mental age of 6.5 was necessary to begin

[4] Mabel V. Morphett and Carleton Washburne, "When Should Children Begin to Read?" *Elementary School Journal*, XXI (March, 1931), pp. 496–503.

reading, there was considerable resistance to this movement. Recently some reading authorities have rendered substantial evidence that children can read at an earlier age. A number of persons and companies have begun to produce teaching materials which purport to teach even babies "to read."

Terman's famous longitudinal study [5] of gifted children produced data which indicated that a significant number of the subjects could read at a very satisfactory level prior to the time they entered school at the first grade level. In fact, one subject could read as well at the age of two years as she could when she started first grade.

One of the most significant needs of the gifted child is that of providing enough challenging reading materials commensurate with his instructional reading level and interests. With this in mind, school authorities need to compile a definite profile of reading interests for each child and provide a large number of books in diverse subject areas. Children identified as gifted need to be placed in common interest groups and provided with various sets of books which represent the predominant reading interests of the pupils involved. Book conferences with the teacher, between pupils and in large group situations are particularly important for these pupils. Verbal interaction should be provided to assure a continuing development of oral language.

Teachers of gifted children should do everything possible to encourage the formation and development of hobbies. For some pupils, a hobby developed during elementary school provides the stimulation for an adult occupation. In one school, the principal and teachers organized a hobby show and invited each child to demonstrate his hobby before the total student body. Most of the projects included in the program originated with gifted and creative students and included such activities as stamp collecting, photo albums, animal and bird specimens, art projects, including ceramics, water color, and oil painting, and antique glasses and furniture. One junior-high boy had spent two years restoring a 1926 Model T Ford.

There should be a considerable amount of re-thinking among

[5] Lewis M. Terman, ed., *Genetic Studies of Genius* (Stanford, Stanford University Press, 1925–1959), Vols. I–V.

educators regarding the amount and kinds of formal reading instruction which should take place during the pre-school and kindergarten years. Creativity should be nourished, since it is during these years that learning takes place at a rapid rate. Once these children reach the first-grade level, they should not be placed in a "lock-step" program with other children. An individualized reading program of either an informal or commercial variety should be used to strengthen developmental reading skills at a pace in relation to the pupil's ability to absorb information.

The experience chart approach may be used with a high degree of success since pupils are encouraged to create their own stories based on everyday experiences. With this method there is a deliberate attempt to get each pupil to pursue oral and written language to his maximum ability. Teachers can use media devices such as films, filmstrips, pictures and instructional television to amplify the language experiences which these children enjoy. Librarians can be asked to cooperate in the endeavor by supplying books and magazines related to the children's interests and abilities.

Critical reading should be stressed with all gifted readers. For example, most will find it challenging and motivating to learn to detect subtle propaganda techniques such as name-calling, bandwagon effect, card-stacking, identification with prestige and personal endorsement. They will become alert to the difference between facts and opinions and whether a given story is mere fantasy or factual. The teacher can encourage critical reading efforts by supplying the pupils with large amounts of reading materials for the purposes outlined previously.

A problem encountered by many gifted pupils is that of social adjustment with their less able peers. Because they are alert and have original ideas, they sometimes become the object of ridicule by other pupils who look upon them as non-conforming and "queer." This attitude places them in a minority resulting in social pressures. Unless the teacher of a heterogeneous group of pupils understands this condition, he may unconsciously tab the gifted child as either a "loner," discipline problem or a disturbing element. There are many unique opportunities available (as described in various parts of this volume) to insure that these undesirable conditions do not form.

Reading Instruction Goals for Gifted Children

Every teacher of gifted children should form a set of instructional goals for reading instruction which are motivational and developmental in nature. These objectives should be somewhat different from those usually established for average children, since the needs and interests of many children at any given chronological age may be divergent. Gifted children should not be placed in any kind of "lock-step" reading program characterized by group instruction procedures. Each child should have an individualized program which will enable him to reach desired objectives (such as those in the following sections) at his own rate. A system of "check-in" and "check-out" tests for each objective might be in order to determine competency.

Reading Competencies for Gifted Children

Word Analysis Skills
The reader should be able to:
1. Recognize a sizeable number of whole words by sight.
2. Employ a number of word analysis tools (phonetic analysis, structural analysis, context clues) in attacking or unlocking unknown words.
3. Use context clues with ease on given words when a difficult word is encountered in instructional level reading material.
4. Select the appropriate phonetic generalization which will aid him in analyzing a given word.
5. Utilize the principles of structural analysis with words which are multisyllabic in nature.
6. Employ the use of different types of dictionaries with special features for word analysis and word meanings.
7. Display some interest in etymology and linguistics in relation to his general interest in word origins.

Comprehension Skills
The reader should be able to:
1. Construct outlines and summaries of paragraphs, chapters or books depending on level of maturity.

2. Grasp the sequence of events and cite the importance of these events when reading selections in such areas as social studies or science.
3. Find important significant details when reading challenging printed materials in such areas as chemistry, physics and mathematics.
4. Differentiate between fact and pure opinion when reading such materials as editorials, books in the behavioral sciences and magazine articles.
5. Predict the outcome of stories and articles based on his past experiences in similar situations.
6. Determine specific types of information from observing maps, charts, graphs, illustrations and pictures.
7. Follow both simple and complex directions from in-class and out-of-class reading assignments and activities.
8. Find the main idea or conclusion in different types of reading materials which are at or above the child's instructional reading level.

Functional Reading Skills
The reader should be able to:
1. Make use of the significant parts of a textbook including the table of contents, index and glossary.
2. Procure various facts and implications from various types of dictionaries, encyclopedias and other source books.
3. Utilize special books of information such as the *World Almanac* and atlases.
4. Use various library sources such as the card catalogue, microfiche library (depending on the age of the person) and the periodicals listings.
5. Interpret diacritical markings, symbols and other markings which are a part of specialized reading sources.

Recreational Reading Skills
The gifted reader will probably:
1. Demonstrate that he reads widely and in a number of sources.
2. Exhibit the desire to want to share information which he has read and enjoyed.

3. Tend to read materials which are at his potential reading level rather than at his instructional reading level.
4. Express a desire to want to engage in creating stories of his own.

Summary

One of the most difficult tasks of dealing with the educational programs of gifted children is that of identification. A number of procedures might be used for this purpose including intelligence tests, achievement tests, informal measures and observation of teachers and administrators. Reading interest inventories can be administered to aid school officials in determining the types of books and materials which should be purchased.

Probably the key person in the identification process is the classroom teacher. The use of a structured form such as the screening and nomination form for creative potential may be particularly useful.

Gifted children need to be challenged and motivated through the use of a wide variety of reading materials. Creativity must be encouraged at every level.

A very carefully structured developmental reading program which includes the components mentioned in the latter part of this chapter is necessary.

CHAPTER II

PRE-READING AND THE PRE-SCHOOL READER

THE FIRST YEAR in school, whether kindergarten or first grade, is usually the beginning of the formalized teaching-learning process for the child. Many different feelings and expectations are held by children about this new venture.

Some children fear school because it means temporarily leaving the protection of the home while others welcome the new adventure and added independence. Some children are timid while others enjoy the social and leadership aspects of the school situation. Some children are unsure of what to expect while others anticipate the rapid acquisition of the skills of reading, writing and adding. Practically all of the children will come to school that first year with a natural curiosity, eagerness and an expectancy to learn. However, learning rates and abilities will vary widely.

At one end of this variance among those school beginners will be gifted children. The general characteristics and learning styles of gifted children were described in Chapter I. Research has indicated a positive correlation between high intelligence and reading ability; studies have shown that one half to one third of all gifted children have developed pre-school reading skills and are reading before starting school. A very early interest and ability in reading have been cited by Hollingworth [1] as indicators of superior intelligence. Terman and Oden [2] also found that reading was one area in which gifted children were superior.

[1] Leta S. Hollingworth, *Gifted Children* (New York, The Macmillan Company, 1906), p. 87.

[2] Lewis M. Terman, and Melita H. Oden, *The Gifted Child Grows Up* (Stanford, Stanford University Press, 1947), p. 28.

Some gifted children may enter school not yet actually reading but on the brink of it, while others, because of environments limited in experiences providing reading prerequisites, may be complete novices in terms of reading skills. In order not to waste the valuable potential of these individuals, early identification of the gifted child is essential. Fox [3] has stated that even kindergarten may begin the cycle of underachievement for gifted children.

Identification

The identification of the gifted youngster is a subject that has occupied experts for some time. Studies, particularly the Hunter College Project, have shown that early identification is possible.

At one time, the individual intelligence test was considered as the most reliable and valid means of disclosing giftedness. More recently, however, these tests have been recognized as being limited by cultural and achievement differences of the children being tested. The tests may be beneficial in some instances as a form of verification. In any case, thorough understanding of the applications and limitations of intelligence tests is essential.

Parents may be considered a source of information in identifying gifted children. Parents cannot be expected to present a completely objective appraisal; however, they can contribute useful insights and background about their child. Checklists, as developed by Brumbaugh and Roscho, [4] provide guidance for parents in viewing their child and describing his abilities and interests. The following is an example of such a checklist:

1. Did your child walk at an unusually early age?
2. Could your child talk plainly at an unusually early age?
3. Was his vocabulary exceptionally large as judged against youngsters of a similar age and sex?
4. Did he demonstrate an exceptional understanding of words?
5. Did he show an early interest in books and being read to?

[3] Ann E. Fox, "Kindergarten: Forgotten Year for the Gifted," *Gifted Child Quarterly*, Vol. XV, No. 1 (Spring, 1971), pp. 42–48.

[4] Florence N. Brumbaugh, and Bernard Roscho, *Your Gifted Child: A Guide for Parents.* (New York: Holt, Rhinehart and Winston, 1959), pp. 43–44.

6. Was he able to identify particular words in books earlier than other children?
7. Did he begin reading before starting school?
8. Was he able to figure out and solve problems of a difficult nature for his age and sex?
9. Did he have unusual imagination for his age?
10. Did he show interest in numbers at an early age?
11. Could he count objects accurately beyond twenty before entering school?
12. Could he count by rote to one hundred before school entrance?
13. Were clocks and calendars of interest to him at an early age?
14. Did he show an early interest in and ability with jigsaw puzzles?
15. Does he have a high level of curiosity and a desire to find answers?
16. Does he enjoy being with children older than himself?
17. Does he have interests or collections that are advanced for his age group?
18. Does he show leadership ability in his own age group?
19. Has he always displayed more stamina than others his age and sex?
20. Do his planning and organizing show exceptional skill and ability?
21. Does he show interest in many things and keep busy?
22. Is he able to apply past learning in new situations?
23. Does he have a longer span of concentration than his peers?
24. Is his sense of humor more highly developed than others his age?
25. Does he pursue difficult problems to their solution?
26. Does he try varied and creative solutions to problems?
27. Does he prefer new and challenging experiences to repetitive and easy ones?
28. Is his memory good?
29. Does he try to achieve high standards of quality in all that he does?

30. Is he aware of his surroundings and able to recall many details about them later?

31. Does he enjoy unusual puzzles and problems?

32. Does he have an exceptional sense of empathy for others?

The teacher has the potential to make effective contributions in the process of detecting giftedness. Even though a consensus has not been reached concerning guidelines, certain traits seem indicative of the gifted individual. The effective classroom teacher should be aware of these characteristics.

A marked degree of competency in vocabulary and verbal skills may be an indication of high intellect; however, caution must be exercised to differentiate between real and superficial ability. Because of exposure to mass communication media, youngsters may have acquired a "talking level" considerably above their understanding.

Drawing cause-effect relationships, exhibiting creativity and questioning behavior, displaying interests at advanced levels, maintaining a prolonged interest span and presenting a measure of self-direction and independence are all traits which denote possibilities of giftedness. Objective observation by teachers should focus also on work habits, problem-solving strategies, deductive-inductive processes, speed in acquisition of understanding, conclusions drawn from abstractions and applications of concepts.

Conforming behavior is not a good indicator; bright youngsters at times are wont to be negative, non-conforming, incessantly questioning and often insistent on pursuit of their own interests.

In order to obtain the most objective and reliable information from observation, the teacher should follow established criteria in a checklist. Suggestions of items other than those suggested for checklists may be found in a variety of reference sources such as Fine,[5] Fliegler [6] and Woolcock.[7]

---

[5] Benjamin Fine, *Stretching Their Minds* (New York, E. P. Dutton and Company, Inc., 1964), pp. 24–32.

[6] Louis A. Fliegler, *Curriculum Planning for the Gifted* (Englewood Cliffs, Prentice-Hall, Inc., 1961), pp. 18–19.

[7] Cyril William Woolcock, *New Approaches to the Education of the Gifted* (Morristown, N. J., Silver Burdett Company, 1961), pp. 45–46.

Though more research is needed in this field, educators must use the best knowledge at hand in order to detect rapid learners as early as possible. Employing a combination of sources and procedures is recommended.

Readiness

The traditional concept of readiness as it found expression in the 1930's related to the idea of maturation. According to this theory, at a certain time, generally a mental age of 6.5 years as specified by Washburne and Morphett, a child had grown or developed to the point that he was ready to learn to read. Up to this time, activities were geared to providing background skills which would prepare the child for the task of reading. As typically applied, these skills were developed with the total group regardless of differences in ability and often centered around common workbooks and duplicated skill sheets. Once a child reached the mental age of 6.5 years, the readiness period was over and learning to read generally was expected to proceed smoothly.

The popularity and general subscription to the readiness theory was attributed by Durkin[8] to the renown of Carleton Washburne, at that time superintendent of the innovative Winnetka, Illinois School System and a leader in the Progressive Education Movement.

The strong adherence to this theory may be attested to even today by its persistence as the practice for beginning reading programs in some schools and school systems. However, among most professional educators today, the meaning of the term "readiness" has become generalized. It is used to refer to the background of understandings needed to facilitate the learning of a new concept in any content area or skill. Readiness is an ongoing consideration that starts at birth and requires utilization throughout life.

Specifically then, readiness as related to reading does not begin and end at the pre-reading level of instruction but is

---

[8] Dolores Durkin, *Teaching Young Children to Read* (Boston, Allyn and Bacon, Inc., 1972), pp. 40–41.

continuous and developed throughout the teaching for acquisition of the reading skills.

Durkin [9] has stated that there is a "relational" aspect of readiness because it depends on the background experience brought to the task by the child and on the methodology employed. Each new concept acquired is a step toward building the next understanding. Based on this modern conception of readiness, the needs of each individual child would be diagnosed and attempted to be met. This is essential for all children if they are to progress and achieve their potential and especially for the gifted child. The old idea that the gifted can learn by themselves is not only unfair and even undemocratic, it is also a serious mistake. These children must be challenged to work to their ability or they may acquire poor study habits early in their lives and eventually become underachievers.

Since the potential of gifted children is greater, they must have opportunity for more extensive and intensive experiences. Gifted children generally need fewer concepts developed at the concrete level and are able to deal with the abstract earlier than other children. Reading, then, is an important skill or tool for the gifted child since books may provide vicarious experiences, thought-provoking ideas and a wealth of information.

The gifted child should be encouraged to develop his reading ability so he can get an early start on acquiring the concepts and knowledge on which further understandings are developed. Proficiency in reading skills affords the gifted child a high degree of independence in learning. He should not be pushed ahead of his needs; neither should he be held back to conform to an arbitrary time-to-learn-to-read schedule. Such schedules may be administratively easier to provide for, less work for teachers in planning and implementing or supportive of a graded-sequential curriculum. However, they have little validity when weighed against the commitment of schools to meet the individual needs of every child. The only time-to-learn-to-read schedule that requires absolute compliance is the one found within each child.

Two other important areas in reading instruction that depend

---

[9] *Ibid.*, p. 51.

on each child are the specific skills in reading that need to be developed and the way in which learning will be facilitated.

Assessment of Reading Skills

Upon school entrance it is important not only to identify children who are gifted; it is also necessary to determine reading abilities. An assessment of the reading skills possessed by a gifted child, including fluency and comprehension of those actually reading, should follow identification. To conduct this assessment, use may be made of standardized reading readiness tests, oral reading tests, teacher-made tests or of selected readings from progressively more difficult trade books or readers with teacher-devised questions or conversation about the material. Having a child read from his own dictated story could also be a good indicator of reading ability. The assessment should extend over several days in order not to tire the child and thus to obtain more valid results.

By using a variety of materials and selections of increasing difficulty in vocabulary and understanding for the child who reads, a teacher may learn about his proficiency or needs in using decoding skills. The teacher may also gain an awareness of the ability of the student to understand what he reads, to make inferences and to use critical thinking.

As an example, the child might be asked to read orally a story such as *The Gingerbread Boy*. This story has a theme developed through a repetitive motif plot structure. After the story has been read, a conversation between child and teacher could utilize such questions as the following:

"Why do you think the gingerbread boy wanted to run away?" (calls for inference based on context)

"Did you think it was right or wrong for him to run away from the little old lady? Why?" (asks for value judgment arrived at through reasoning)

"Could you think of someone else he might have met and run away from? Perhaps you could add your idea to the story and tell it as a part of the story. Where in the story would you place your idea—after what or before what?" (requires awareness of plot structure and understanding of story)

In addition to the preceding method, stories dealing with progressively unfamiliar realms could yield valuable information about the ability of a child and the extensiveness of his background.

A general competency chart is recommended as a device for recording the reading skill each gifted child possesses at the time of the initial assessment. The information such a chart gives is limited, but it will provide a rapid identification of general reading needs. An example of a general competency chart is shown in Table I.

As indicated by the comments on the chart concerning the acquired skills of each of the gifted children shown, the following assumptions about reading ability can be made:

Susan has been identified through a variety of means as being gifted, but she is lacking many of the skills necessary for reading.

James apparently has learned to read on his own before entry to school, but he needs additional development in the area of critical reading skills.

Billy has acquired some of the basic skills and appears to know some words, which shows his interest in reading. He could be assessed as being on the verge of learning to read.

Suggestions for guiding the reading skill development of gifted youngsters at each of the general stages as depicted by those on the chart will be presented later in this chapter.

After the initial assessment information has been gained and instruction as indicated has begun, more detailed checklists should be prepared to provide the teacher with better information in terms of specific skill needs and attainments. This type could be designed to make an individual record to accompany the child throughout the entire period of his acquisition of reading skills. Such a checklist makes diagnostic teaching possible. For this checklist, sections should be included for word recognition skills, comprehension skills, critical reading skills and study skills. All of the basic skills under each heading should be identified and marked off as the child shows mastery.

The child who demonstrates proficiency in decoding symbols accurately should not be expected to participate in pre-reading activities. If a child is able to "work out" the pronunciation of

TABLE I

GENERAL COMPETENCY CHART OF THE READING SKILLS AND ABILITIES OF THE GIFTED

Names	Skills and Abilities								
	Visual Perception	Audio Perception	Left to Right Sequence	Word Recognition	Pronunciation	Phrasing	Para-language	Compre-hension	Critical Reading
Susan	Needs de-tail work	Can't find close differ-ences	Sporadic	Knows name	Clear in speaking	—	—	Good when read to	Recognized character traits
James	Fine	Fine	Has mastery	Able to de-code most words	Usually accurate	Good	Pitch and stress need development	Excellent	More work on cause-effect skills
Billy	Fine	Fine	Has mastery	Difficulty with new words	Fine with known words, others difficult	General lack	Needs work Applies periods	When read to—very good	Makes simple inferences

etc.

new words most of the time, it would seem apparent that the child has integrated his own successful system of decoding. Unless a definite and specific need is shown by such a child, word analysis skills would not be included in his learning plans at this level and would be marked off on his individual checklist as already acquired. It must be remembered, particularly in terms of the gifted child, that reading is a skill and must not be treated as a content area.

Reading instruction would consist of individual sessions with the classroom teacher or a reading teacher to aid the development of necessary diagnosed skills in word analysis, comprehension, and study skills. If well-planned and paced, this session could involve as little time as ten to fifteen minutes a day for kindergartners or fifteen to twenty minutes a day for first graders. The pace of instruction as well as the concepts to be developed and strategies used must be geared to the student. It must be remembered that the gifted child is a rapid learner. If these children are kept in regular groups, they will not be stimulated to their ability or to a reasonable effort, often resulting in boredom and the acquisition of poor study habits. Very bright children as well as the slow learners may mentally become school dropouts at an early age.

The Child Who Reads on Entry to School

For the child who enters school as a reader, plans should consist of experiences such as those which follow.

Since silent reading will be a prime source of learning for the gifted individual throughout his life, it is important to provide the child with ample opportunity, help and materials to read. Understanding should be checked periodically through conversation with the pupil about his reading. Basal readers as well as trade books could be used.

After silent reading, minimum amounts of oral or interpretative reading are needed only to check and guide the appropriate use of paralanguage skills (stress, pitch and juncture) as an aid to comprehension.

Strategies to develop these skills could include ideas such as the following:

"Read this sentence (phrase or paragraph) in the way in which you think ＿＿＿＿＿＿ would have said it."

"How would you read these words in bold type?"

"Read this sentence to show what the exclamation mark means."

For demonstration, the teacher could read the same sentence in different ways in terms of paralanguage. Follow-up questions could be:

"Was there a difference in meaning? What kind of difference?"

Such activities may also be used to aid locational skills, skimming and scanning. Oral reading will aid the discovery of possible needs in word analysis skills.

For the bright child, critical reading skills should be introduced and developed along with the acquisition of decoding skills and fluency. As with the majority of children, it is necessary to begin with the simple skills and move on through the increasing stages of complexity. However, pacing for the gifted will generally be more rapid and some skills may require little attention because of proficiency.

Character study may begin with what a person has done or said and move into the realm of inferring why the character acted or spoke as he did. Further areas of inference could center on what kind of person this is as implied by the story.

Cause-effect relationships could be developed through predicting what will happen next or how the story will end based on what has already been read. Children can learn to infer and predict from pictures as well as from context.

Learning to differentiate real from unreal in settings, characters and plots may be developed with questions such as: "Tell us why you think this story really could or could not happen?"

Gifted children can begin to identify simple plot structures and even make comparisons of the plots of two stories.

The nature and maturity of the skills presented to any child will depend on the ability of the individual. Upper levels of gifted children will be able to progress to greater depths of thinking and analysis in critical reading skills than often assumed. Such youngsters need to be stimulated and challenged so they will not become lazy in their thinking habits. Surface questions with expected answers require little thought or real mental activity. Creative questioning is an art and requires a creative teacher.

The Child Ready to Read

Many gifted children will enter school not yet reading but ready to begin. These youngsters generally have developed the basic decoding skills and can identify some words and phrases. As with the child who enters school already reading, the reading assessment will provide direction for planning experiences according to the needs and abilities of each individual. Often it is merely encouragement, a minimum of basic skills and the opportunity for practice which must be supplied to such children.

The language experience approach in which the child dictates his story and reads it back could be a beneficial strategy to develop further the reading skills. Through this technique, confidence and security may be built as the child works within his own vocabulary, syntactical patterns and experiences.

There are many ways in which children may be stimulated to write or dictate stories or poems. The following ideas are cited as examples:

1. Carefully contrived interest centers could serve as a source of stimulation for the dictated story or poem.
2. The child could view simple filmstrip stories without sound and dictate a story or poem to be read later to other children in accompaniment to the filmstrip.
3. The child could supply the ending or an alternative ending for a story or poem read to him. With teacher aid he then could read the completed work for enjoyment.
4. After hearing a selection read to a group, a child could contrive a parallel story or poem. Creative development may be aided greatly by reading wide varieties of stories and poems.
5. The child could interpret his own or another picture and dictate his own creative piece about it to be read later.
6. Field trips, seeing and listening walks and other class or individual activity experiences could be used to elicit written creative expression by children.

In using the language experience technique, it is important

that the story or poem be written exactly as the child dictates it.

With the growth of confidence and fluency, reading experiences could be expanded to published materials in which the vocabulary, language patterns and experiences will be more varied and perhaps new. A variety of easily accessible trade books of interest to the child will aid further development of the reading skills. To promote independence in the use of these books, a picture dictionary will prove quite helpful.

Cassette tapes or records of stories with the accompanying book provide to the child the opportunity of following the printed words as he hears the story. This can be a valuable experience in several ways: the child learns new vocabulary, gains exposure to a variety of language patterns, has an added degree of independence in learning and has the opportunity to enjoy good literature.

As soon as he is ready, the child should be advanced to the type of activities described for the gifted student who enters school already reading.

The Child Who Enters School with Little or No Reading Skill

Because of a lack of background conducive to building necessary reading prerequisites, some gifted children will enter school with little or no reading skill. Any abilities possessed should be noted in the assessment and recorded for added development as a starting place to begin building reading skills.

For gifted children in this category, pre-reading activities and experiences are necessary prior to teaching reading skills. However, it is important to re-emphasize the fact that gifted children are rapid learners; therefore, they should not be slowed down to work in whole classes or with groups of less gifted. The individual learning pace of a gifted child must be met. This does not preclude the possibility of presenting commonly needed experiences or skills to a small group of gifted, after which practice or development for mastery could be accomplished in a group, with a partner or individually. This plan relies upon the concept of flexible groupings based upon the diagnosed needs of each student.

Varied and creative language experiences are highly recommended as a form of pre-reading activity since language facility is important to acquiring reading skills. The child needs exposure to many real and literary experiences to provide sources for verbal reactions. The opportunity for a broad background in vocabulary, language manipulation and general knowledge increases with the breadth and depth, as well as quality, of experiences offered.

Such experiences may utilize the following suggestions depending upon the child's needs. In each the teacher serves as stimulator, facilitator, questioner, listener and positive reinforcer but not as the source of knowledge.

1. Use interest centers which involve a high degree of creative manipulation of materials. Informal conversations could encourage the child to explain what he tried and why. Step-by-step procedures to show relational sequences could be developed by the gifted child with guidance.

2. Articles could be put into containers in which the child handles the object without seeing it, then describes it to the group to identify. Children should be urged and helped to use the most pertinent descriptive words and phrases in their report to the others, as examples:

   round, flat sides, hard, metal, small—coin
   round all over, soft, rubber, fist size—ball

   In the beginning, descriptively different materials could be used; as skill progresses the items included may share some common properties which would require greater specificity in their description. Those involved in the identification of the object should be guided toward careful listening and consideration of the words and phrases to prevent random guessing and to ask relevant questions. With direction, gifted children will become proficient in this activity fairly rapidly.

3. Field trips to places of interest could arouse multiple language opportunities in the preparation for, during and as follow-up after the trip. For those gifted youngsters who have had little or no acquaintance with the world outside the few blocks surrounding their home and school, these outings are essential. Every community provides a wealth

of places for visits, such as a zoo, a botanical garden, an office building, a park with trees and shrubs, a farm or a library.

4. Walks may be arranged to satisfy different purposes. Tours of the school building with opportunities to meet and talk to people who work in the school could promote many possibilities for language utilization. A walk in the immediate neighborhood with pre-determined goals for listening or for looking would provide a wealth of material about which to discuss, describe and perhaps tell stories.

5. Experiences in hearing good stories and poetry often are excellent means of exposing children to language. If well-chosen, these materials can provide beneficial examples of the use and value of words through trying informal techniques with occasional selections such as: "Show us how the child went down the street. Why did you choose that way? What word did the story use to tell you? Can you think of other words to use that would change how the child might go down the street?" Caution must be urged that the story and pleasure derived from it must not be ruined by over-analysis.

6. Storytelling by the teacher may be a way to create an interest in participating in telling stories they enjoyed.

7. Creative dramatics could follow a story that a group has heard and enjoyed.

8. Some stories may stimulate themes for creative play activities.

9. Choral interpretation may take the form of joining in repeated lines or reciting the entire poem or selection with the group.

10. Literature also has the quality of providing vicarious experiences which most gifted children assimilate easily.

11. Carefully selected records, films and filmstrips, whether of literature or pertaining to other topics, can be good language stimulators when used by master teachers.

12. Certain offerings on educational television could be useful if carefully and creatively programmed and properly introduced and followed up in the classroom.

A fairly easy and fast analysis will indicate other types of experiences a gifted child in this category will need. The amount of time devoted to such enterprises would be based on indicated deficiencies and direct value of the experience. Time spent on any skill already acquired and put into application becomes busy work and a waste of the talents of a gifted child.

A sample list of areas which could affect reading success and may require checking for proficiency is suggested:

1. *Visual perception.* Included could be such skills as: simple identification, close proximity matching, reproduction of a distant model, recognizing varieties of likenesses and differences and identifying repeated patterns as opposed to random patterns.

2. *Audio perception.* This could deal with abilities as: accurately hearing and following directions, reproducing words and phrases and repeating simple tongue twisters and nonsense words.

3. *Left to right sequence.* This requires complete mastery as shown through such activities as: counting rows of objects, identifying ordinal positions of articles in a sequence, telling a story from a series of ordered illustrations or placing objects in a variety of sequential organizations.

These suggestions are by no means meant to be all inclusive or confining to the creative teacher; they are offered to stimulate thought, direction and imagination in the teacher working with one or several gifted children.

As the child indicates interest in the printed word and the desire to read, he should be aided and encouraged to continue to learn in accordance with his potential. Several strategies are available at this stage for the teacher to use: language experience, basal reader, modified basal reader or individualization with trade books. It might be feasible to try more than one method or combination in order to allow maximum progress for the child.

In general, word analysis skill development may require more attention for the gifted child with a background meager in reading prerequisites. Certain basic skills may require study, but they should not be prolonged after meaningful application occurs and pacing should not lag behind the ability of the individual. Again, diagnosed skill needs are those that are taught.

Word Recognition Skills

Any essential skills insufficient to develop the reading fluency of a particular student must be taught. Generally, the teaching and practice of a skill will require a minimum amount of time. No more time need be spent on a skill when it has been assimilated into the decoding system of the rapid-learning child.

Decisions concerning what skills should be taught to a certain child may be based on the objective of correcting any consistent difficulties discovered during oral or silent reading. When a problem area is found, the teacher should guide the child into an awareness of the specific need. Then through joint effort, objectives and plans may be made. Through understanding the need and working out general plans with the teacher, the gifted child may acquire a sense of responsibility for his own learning early in life.

There will be instances in which two or more children are deficient in the same skill area. For efficiency the teacher would present experiences to develop understanding and reinforce the necessary skill to a group requiring it and ready for it. Creative activities would be prescribed on the basis of exhibited need for individual or partner work. If indicated, the group, excluding those who have achieved mastery since the last meeting, would be brought together again for further explanation and application of the skill.

Often it will be found that the gifted youngster will require individual attention because of his rapid pace of learning and unique needs.

Demonstrated competencies should be marked off on the individual skills checklist discussed previously so that the record is always accurate and up to date.

Study Skills

The early acquisition of study skills for the rapid learner is essential since these are the skills which give the child increased independence in learning.

The first year in school is not too early to begin guiding the gifted in the use of these skills. The values and uses of such aids as a dictionary for beginners, a table of contents, a simple index and topic headings should be developed and reinforced.

These skills become very meaningful through the use of non-fiction, informational books to answer questions or to add further to a topic under discussion.

As an example, the interest center may be the source of motivation. Because of experiences provided by the interest center, questions may be raised by children about rationales for processes or related areas of interest. Need situations of this kind provide the ideal teaching opportunity as the use and value of a table of contents, topic headings and an index become evident. If not forthcoming from children, some questions may be teacher-initiated in order to develop certain study skills. These questions must not be token questions; for effective learning they must be well-thought out and of real pertinence to the interest center topic.

Although this may appear to the uninitiated to be incidental teaching, this form of integrated learning requires careful thought and planning.

Materials

Interest Centers. The need for interest centers exists for all children throughout their school experiences as well as during the first year in school.

There may be permanent interest centers for areas as science and math, while other centers will focus on various interests for a short period of time and then will be changed to explore different topics. By including a variety of types and levels of materials, objects and books all children will benefit. Materials and books which the gifted child will find interesting and challenging will further encourage him to question, search and experiment. His curiosity must be aroused and encouraged to retain his enthusiasm for learning.

Combined with picture and picture-story books dealing with related subjects, many of the books used for interest centers should be of the informational or non-fiction category.

A well-planned interest center can provide for more integrated learning experiences than one hastily put together. Even though certain learning goals may be planned for consciously, this does not preclude peripheral and extemporaneous learning emanating from the naturally curious and inventive minds of children. Goals of the interest center should be established and it should be organized to meet these objectives.

A plan for a science interest center about sound follows.

SCIENCE INTEREST CENTER
SOUND

General Objectives:

Through the use of a variety of materials in the interest center, the child will be able to demonstrate his understanding of the principles of the production of high and low tones by:

1. First telling and then demonstrating from several glasses filled with water his selection of those that will produce: (a) the highest pitched tone and (b) the lowest pitched tone.
2. Stretching rubber bands around golf tees on a peg board to produce: (a) high pitched tones and (b) low pitched tones.
3. Selecting and demonstrating with tuning forks those that produce: (a) the highest pitched tones, (b) the lowest pitched tones, and (c) the medium pitched tones.
4. Predicting after examination which strings on a guitar will produce: (a) the highest pitched tone and (b) the lowest pitched tone.

Materials:

—Four identical water glasses with colored water in varied amounts to produce four different tones.
—Three or four twelve-inch square peg boards, two dozen wooden golf tees, rubber bands of varied widths, lengths and tension capabilities.
—Three tuning forks of different pitches
—Guitar (toy or real)
—Books:

The True Book of Sounds We Hear by Illa Podendorf [10]
High Sounds, Low Sounds by Franklyn M. Branley [11]
Sounds All Around by Tillie S. Pine and Joseph Levine [12]
Sound by Lisa Miller [13]
Sound by Solveig Paulson Russell [14]

The preceding is an example of a very basic interest center. Children can bring more ideas and materials to the center. An interest center so conceived as to allow for experimentation and discovery can provide stimulation, especially for the gifted, to turn to the books displayed in order to gain more information. Through such means, reading is demonstrated as a necessary skill.

NEWSPAPERS FOR CHILDREN. Weekly "newspapers" for children are available at various reading ability levels. Selection of these materials should be made commensurate with skills and needs.

TRADE BOOKS. Gifted children require access to the school library and library books. They must be allowed adequate browsing time to make their selections to take home. Guidance should be available and provided upon request by the child.

Library books checked out to the classroom should be readily available for use and changed regularly. The room collection should be varied in terms of content and reading difficulty. A dictionary for beginners kept on hand could be highly beneficial to the fast learner.

Gifted children can increase their reading ability further through the use of previously mentioned recorded or taped stories which accompany books. These audio materials may be purchased or they may be made very easily by the teacher.

FILMED MATERIALS. There is a variety of commercially produced films, filmstrips and film loops reproducing good litera-

[10] Illa Podendorf, *The True Book of Sounds We Hear* (Chicago, Children's Press, 1955).

[11] Franklyn M. Branley, *High Sounds, Low Sounds* (New York, Thomas Y. Crowell Company, 1967).

[12] Tillie S. Pine, and Joseph Levine, *Sounds All Around* (New York, McGraw-Hill Book Company, 1958).

[13] Lisa Miller, *Sound* (New York, Coward McCann, Inc., 1965).

[14] Solveig Paulson Russell, *Sound* (Indianapolis, Bobbs-Merrill Company, Inc., 1963).

ture for children which could be used creatively in working with the gifted.

CREATIVE PLAY EQUIPMENT. This equipment consists of anything and everything in order to pique the imagination. Suggested or demonstrated uses should be prohibited; instead children should be allowed to discover the materials and innovate with them. These experiences abound with language possibilities.

Summary

Identification of gifted youngsters is imperative as soon after their initial school entry as possible. An assessment of reading ability will give the teacher direction in planning and guiding learning experiences for such children.

Readiness as formerly viewed was based on the theory that when a child reached his maturation level, later arbitrarily set at the age of 6.5 years, he would be ready to read. Current theory considers readiness as a continuous process throughout life in which acquired understandings and experiences provide the bases for learning new concepts. There is no magic age to learn to read; it varies with each child.

For the child who enters school reading, the main goal should be to give him the freedom and guidance to use his self-acquired skill in pursuit of greater depth and broader extension of his interests.

Encouragement, the teaching of requisite basic skills and provision for reading experiences form the basis of the reading program for the gifted child on the verge of reading when he enters school.

Carefully selected pre-reading activities and basic skill experiences are necessary for the rapid learner who has begun his school years lacking the prerequisites essential to developing the skill of reading.

Comprehension and critical reading ability must receive the major emphasis in reading instruction for gifted children. Other reading skills are presented when needed to enhance understanding and interpretation.

As the gifted child develops his own decoding system, only

those word recognition skills detected as deficiencies hindering the reading fluency of the youngster need to be taught.

Study skills enable the gifted child to enjoy greater independence in pursuit of learning and developing his own interests. Therefore, these skills should be presented to a child as early and as rapidly as he can assimilate them.

Since the first year of school often sets learning patterns and habits, it is imperative that the gifted child be given individual attention with curriculum plans based on his unique needs and learning rate.

ORGANIZING FOR
INSTRUCTION

THE ORGANIZATION DESIGNS for the elementary school are classified under the general headings of vertical and horizontal. Vertical patterns of organization are graded or nongraded with great diversity exhibited in each. Horizontal plans are those that deal with organizational schemes at one grade or level.

The earliest schools in this country enrolled few students and functioned in a nongraded pattern. However, as education gained more importance and as the number of students increased, grouping through a graded structure based on chronological age was adopted as a means to alleviate the problem of teaching such large, diverse groups. Curricula were designed to accompany the graded organization pattern, with implementation often becoming a "lock-step" process.

Efforts to eliminate the rigidity of graded structures focused again on the theory of nongradedness. Unfortunately, as actually practiced in many places there was little to distinguish it from the graded school other than in terminology used. Curricula and methodology generally remained unchanged.

As interest in the gifted grew, it became apparent that the normal fare offered by the schools was insufficient for them. Through endeavors to provide for the special learning needs of high ability youngsters, modifications within the graded structure have been proposed and used. Basically, the changes most often prescribed were alterations of the existing programs and came under the categories of acceleration, ability grouping and enrichment.

In this chapter, an attempt has been made to summarize and describe selected organizational patterns which have been put to use to teach reading to the gifted. A brief discussion about teachers of the gifted will also be included.

Vertical Patterns

Ability grouping and acceleration have been suggested most often as the recommended modes for adjusting vertical organizational patterns to the particular learning needs of the gifted. Since vertical organization patterns basically are determined for administrative purposes, reading and the content areas generally receive no special consideration in their formulation.

Ability Grouping

The debate over ability grouping has been carried on for years. Because research in this area has been inconclusive, opinions and emotions generally have formed the basis for the pro and con sentiments. Objections have been raised that ability grouping is a form of segregation which may cause feelings of superiority and give unfair educational opportunities to the few. In rebuttal, it has been contended that natural segregation and integration tend to occur regardless of the organizational pattern and that "sameness" in education is undemocratic if, in truth, the educational objective of helping each child develop to his full potential is pursued. Proponents claim the use of ability grouping increases the capability of the school to improve the learning possibilities for the gifted. Provision for extra subject matter, perhaps even extra subjects, is more nearly possible. Better work habits and greater motivation may be outcomes of grouping together children with similar mental ability. Objections to this scheme of providing for the gifted tend to portray it as a superficial remedy, since regardless of how groups are selected, more heterogeneity than homogeneity will exist. The lack of homogeneity may be forgotten when ability groupings are utilized.

MENTAL AGE. In conjunction with vertical arrangements, grouping is used particularly to reduce the broad range of ability in any one classroom. One possibility to accomplish this is to group by mental age rather than by chronological age. In terms of teaching reading, this would allow the younger gifted child to work with concepts and materials more closely related to his ability in reading. However, the problems outweigh any possible advantages. Even complete grouping by mental age will not eliminate the differences in the groups. Gifted youngsters are fast learners and generally grasp concepts more quickly and with less need for concrete or substantive teaching strategies than the average older child with the same mental age. Specific reading skill needs and interests would continue to be widely varied. Using one factor such as mental age for the only criterion for grouping is no solution.

UNGRADED ROOM. The ungraded room is another attempt at adjustment. Plans of this type may call for grouping children from several grades together in a manner somewhat reminiscent of the one-room schoolhouse. It does allow for a child to work on his own needs with the added feature of joining older children in pursuit of similar interests or needs. Critical reading skills and study skills particularly could be enhanced through this association. To be most effective, individualized reading instruction would be needed as the nucleus of this program. Social factors could be a cause for concern in this type of grouping if the chronological age range is too great.

CONTINUOUS PROGRESS. A similar concept is the continuous progress design. Again, a plan of individualized reading would be needed as the basis if the greatest potential is to be reached in teaching reading skills in such a design. Monroe and Rogers [1] pointed out, ". . . the pupil is assigned to special small groups according to his readiness level in specific content or skill areas." This type of organization permits greater flexibility of grouping. The continuous progress concept would eliminate the graded structure by bringing together an extended age unit (i.e. primary or intermediate levels). Each youngster would pursue his own diagnosed reading needs at his own learning rate. The skills and concepts in such a plan are arranged in a sequenced order of difficulty often called levels. A child may complete these levels at his own pace. This plan may reduce or remove the occasional

[1] Marion Monroe and Bernice Rogers, *Foundations for Reading: Informal Pre-Reading Procedures* (Chicago, Scott, Foresman and Company, 1964), p. 197.

stigma associated with rapid learners or slow learners. Grouping in this manner also allows for integration of age and ability levels within a primary or intermediate unit which, in a positive setting, could be extremely helpful in the social development of a gifted child. There are many enriching reading experiences and activities that children with similar interests but differing abilities can enjoy and learn from together.

JOPLIN PLAN. A form of ability grouping for reading used with a variety of modifications is the Joplin Plan. For reading classes, children are grouped schoolwide according to achievement levels. This arrangement conceivably could bring together children of widely divergent chronological ages while still retaining a heterogeneous group in terms of specific reading abilities and needs. It would offer gifted youngsters the advantage of being able to work with others of a similar mental age, but as pointed out earlier, widely different capacities are possessed by gifted children and average children of the same mental age. Groups within the primary grades are formed separately from the groups within the intermediate grades in an attempt to control the range of chronological ages in a class for social reasons. Another adaptation of this plan will be discussed later in this chapter under horizontal patterns.

Acceleration

As defined by Ward [2] acceleration is, "any administrative practice designed to move the student through school more rapidly than usual." Included under the general title are such measures as grade skipping, early admission, rapid progress classes, credit by examination at the higher levels, and advanced placement.

Stress has been put upon the desirability of moving gifted young people through the formal educative process as rapidly as possible in order for them to concentrate sooner on their special interests or careers. Much of the concern to reduce the time spent in school by high ability young people is due to the results

[2] Virgil S. Ward, "Basic Concepts," in Walter B. Barbe, ed., *Psychology and Education of the Gifted: Selected Readings* (New York, Appleton-Century-Crofts, 1965), p. 49.

of biographical studies conducted by Lehman,[3] who found that most creative contributions were made by people in their early adult years, with the peak occurring during the thirties.

Based on research findings, experts in the field have advocated the general concept of acceleration as a means of adjusting the regular school pattern for the rapid learner. Woolcock[4] stated, "Gifted students cannot, in the main, be adequately challenged and held attentive without some acceleration of the educational process." According to Freehill,[5] "Research findings show positive outcomes from acceleration and seem to argue for much greater differentials in rate of progress through the schools."

Regardless of the research evidence and support for acceleration, it has been an adaptive approach which has found limited implementation.

EARLY ADMISSION. Early admission to school is one form of acceleration that has been accepted rather widely. When children have been carefully selected and at the time of school entrance found to be superior in terms of social, emotional and physical maturity and reading aptitude, DeHaan and Havighurst[6] reported that studies have shown early admission of children far below the age of five years seven months has been successful. In fact, Gold[7] stated projects and studies have shown early admission as a definite advantage for bright children. They tended to achieve better throughout school and suffered no ill effects socially or emotionally. When placed from the beginning with youngsters who are closer to being his mental equals, the gifted child will receive more intellectual stimulation than with chronological age mates. Important reading skills could be developed sooner, thus providing the child with a tool to broaden

[3] Harvey Lehman, *Age and Achievement* (Princeton, N. J., Princeton University Press, Copyright by American Philosophical Society, 1953).

[4] Cyril William Woolcock, *New Approaches to the Education of the Gifted* (Morristown, N. J., Silver Burdett Company, 1961), p. 28.

[5] Maurice F. Freehill, *Gifted Children—Their Psychology and Education* (New York, The Macmillan Co., 1961), p. 195.

[6] Robert DeHaan and Robert J. Havighurst, *Educating Gifted Children* (Chicago, The University of Chicago Press, 1957), p. 124.

[7] Milton J. Gold, *Education of the Intellectually Gifted* (Columbus, Ohio, Charles E. Merrill Books, Inc., 1965), p. 335.

his learning scope at an earlier age. Although the expense of testing, selection of adequate methods and materials for identifying gifted children and administrative complications act as hindrances to this concept, many school systems have made provisions for its use.

GRADE SKIPPING. Another form of acceleration is grade skipping. The double promotion is probably the most expedient and inexpensive method of dealing with the gifted. The possible emotional and adjustment problems resulting from this practice have been pointed out by Witty,[8] but emotionally stable youngsters will not be hurt by skipping a grade or two if it is done early in the elementary years. This plan allows the student to move more rapidly through school and finish earlier as well as challenging his intellectual abilities by working with those of a similar mental age. In terms of reading, importance is placed on the selection of those young people to be accelerated in this manner. Care must be taken to determine that the reading skills of the child are advanced enough to adjust to the higher level. Where a double promotion has been effected, the teacher must be vigilant in checking to discover needed reading skills which may have been missed. These youngsters invariably are fluent readers which indicates proficiency in decoding skills, but this proficiency must not be generalized to other areas. The major skills to assess lie in the categories of comprehension, study skills and critical reading. Through the years, this particular form of acceleration has received much criticism and little use.

RAPID PROGRESS. A more acceptable variation of grade skipping is the faster paced or rapid progress concept. With this plan the gifted child, because of his rapid learning abilities, is usually expected to complete the basic requirements of two grades in one year in order to advance to a higher grade. This idea was conceived to avoid the gaps of double promotion. Obviously curricular revisions and instructional changes would be required. The implementation of this concept varies from expecting a classroom teacher to make all of the necessary provisions, to the

---

[8] Paul Witty, *Helping the Gifted Child* (Chicago, Science Research Associates, Inc., 1952), p. 39.

creation of special classes into which children are moved for a year in order to acquire the skills for academic adjustment. This could be explained as a plan in which gifted children are asked to speed up their learning pace to get to the next grade level, then after reaching it, to slow down again to suit the pace of the average child.

Horizontal Patterns

In making adjustments for the gifted on a horizontal basis, two basic types of provisions are attempted through ability grouping and enrichment. Skill areas and subject areas may be planned for specifically in measures employed within grades or levels.

Ability Grouping

HOMOGENEOUS GROUPING. Total homogeneous grouping may involve separating all of the students at each grade level into classes in which all have similar levels of ability. In cities where the school population is large enough, it could mean designating a whole school for children of superior ability. It may also be used to refer to the practice of creating separate classes for gifted within a comprehensive school. The basis on which youngsters are selected for these groups may present difficulties. A single factor must not be used to make grouping decisions. Besides academic ability, concern must be shown for factors as social and emotional development, motivation, interest and attitude. Reading instruction may be facilitated in this organizational structure by providing more challenging materials and intellectual stimulation. Freehill[9] stated, "Gifted children unchallenged tend to read widely but not beyond the level of their classmates. They are articulate but shallow."

For homogeneous grouping to be effective, Gold[10] has specified that changes in curriculum, methods and materials must occur. This would apply most definitely to reading, especially in the need for development of abstract and critical reading skills

[9] Freehill, *op. cit.*, p. 195.
[10] Gold, *op. cit.*, p. 304.

in greater depth. A basic concern regarding grouping of this kind is that any group is characterized more by differences than by likenesses. Regardless of similarities with others in mental age or reading achievement level, each individual will have deficiencies, proficiencies, interests and a learning rate exclusively his own.

MODIFIED ABILITY GROUPING. Modified ability grouping is used as a general term to include a variety of practices. In some instances, it involves a divided day structure in which some activities are carried on with the whole class and the other areas, often skill and some content areas, are taught in special groupings or classes. While some modifications are centered around the "core" idea for special grouping, other designs use special interests as the basis for organization. Another adaptation is the released time approach. Since gifted children generally work faster, they are dismissed during some of the day or for a limited number of periods during the week for special activities.

An arrangement specifically for reading is a modification of the Joplin Plan. For this, grade lines are not crossed, but it would require that a school have at least two (preferably three) sections of a grade level. The children from all sections are grouped according to reading achievement and move to the appropriate room each day for reading class. While this reduces the achievement span somewhat in a class, it will not eliminate the individual differences in abilities and acquired skills within a group.

For many years, probably the most extensively used form of ability grouping has been in-class grouping which became a common practice for the teaching of reading. Three is the arbitrarily set number of reading groups most often recommended for a regular class with one teacher. This plan calls upon the teacher to vary the rate of progress, difficulty of materials and teaching strategies for each group. Problems with this arrangement arise if the groups become fixed in membership or if the children are taught as a unit rather than as individuals. Flexible groupings must be employed within this basic structure for any effective treatment of specific skill needs.

Enrichment

As a means of meeting the academic needs of the youngster with superior ability enrichment has been the most acceptable and widely used method. Intensive or in-depth enrichment is based on the interests of a child and allows him to study a topic more deeply than normally expected. For some gifted students this form of enrichment, if used exclusively, may be too limiting and narrow. Variety and wide exploration in order to develop as many of the abilities of the learner as possible are features of extensive or in-breadth enrichment. Total dependence on this plan for enrichment could produce young people with a broad but shallow field of knowledge and no understanding of the basic skills employed in research. A balanced plan will provide for both types of enrichment in order to expand the background of the gifted and still meet their needs and interests.

Enrichment must not be interpreted as meaning more of the same kind of activities and lessons. To be effective, enrichment plans must be well thought out and comprehensive. Curricular revisions are essential to give direction and to guard against inclusions of bits and pieces of little value and omissions of essential skills. Pursuit of individual interests is not only possible within this framework but forms a part of the program for the gifted.

There may be a variety of arrangements made for enrichment purposes.

REGULAR CLASSROOM. Even though it may refer to all of the adjustments made for the gifted, the common interpretations of enrichment often are considered to be those arrangements made in the regular classroom. This is probably the least controversial method of providing for the superior learner and does not necessitate a change in the organizational structure of the school. The practices usually employed in reading are to form a small group of these children for an in-breadth approach or to follow an individualized reading plan which might provide some breadth and depth. A variety of types of activities is used in making provisions for gifted in the regular classroom.

1. *Special Assignments.* The child participates in the regular class work but his assignments are more difficult.
2. *Projects.* Projects may be organized as individual or group activities. When working with the group, the gifted child may be assigned work that requires more in-depth research or he may serve in a leadership role.
3. *Free Choice Activity.* In place of a lesson in which the child already has demonstrated competency or after he has completed an assignment, the rapid learner would be allowed to select a project or activity of interest to pursue on his own.
4. *Monitor and Demonstrator.* This is a dubious practice in which the bright child is used to assist other students with questions or difficulties or to help the teacher with record keeping and similar tasks. The youngster is kept busy and other children may profit from the extra help provided, but it cheats the gifted one from developing his abilities and interests.
5. *Contract Plan.* The student signs a contract in which he assumes responsibility for completing a specified unit of work or certain activity in a stated period of time. If used meaningfully and not as busy work this plan provides for individual learning and allows the child to work at his own rate.

RELEASED TIME. Arrangements may be made for superior ability children from regular classrooms to have released time each day or for certain periods during the week to devote to individual interests such as a comparison of classical myths to "pourquoi" stories or perhaps to increase reading speed. For such a plan to be really effective, a well equipped media-center library with resource aid available is necessary.

HOBBY AND CLUB PLANS. Reading hobby groups or interest clubs may include youngsters from one class, from within grade levels, or from across grade lines. Participation is based on interest and may not be limited to the gifted. An exceptional teacher with this same interest should be the leader or sponsor of such a group or club.

SPECIAL CLASSES. Special enrichment classes in reading may be scheduled before or after school or on Saturday for bright youngsters. Topics and the treatment of such would be extensive and intensive and selected for study by either a group or individual. Again, an outstanding teacher is necessary.

SUMMER SCHOOL. Enrichment in reading through special offerings in summer programs has been made available by some school systems. For young children who have been identified as gifted but who are lacking reading prerequisites, a carefully planned but informally conducted summer program comprised of literature and pre-reading activities could be extremely beneficial. Class size must be kept small if any real accomplishments are made.

COMMUNITY RESOURCES. The public library is one of the most valuable resources in any community, especially to the gifted child. With mutual cooperation and planning between school and library, a regularly scheduled program of literature and library skills development could be presented during school hours at the library. This idea has been used in some cities and has proven to be a rich source of knowledge and enjoyment.

In Retrospect

Ability grouping whether carried out vertically, horizontally or in combination is no panacea in itself. If it is believed that once the groupings have been formed learning differences have been met, the scheme actually becomes a negative force in the educative process. Based on the situation and a combination of factors such as the attitudes of all involved, the curricular adjustment and the use of diverse teaching strategies, forms of ability grouping could produce positive results as an arrangement for meeting needs of the gifted.

The success of acceleration when practiced through grade skipping or early admission is dependent upon the person selected. If emotionally, socially and academically able, acceleration will not harm the child but will allow him to finish school at an earlier age. Both double promotion and early admission may serve the purpose of placing the gifted child with those nearer to him in mental age but he is still expected to move through a program designed for the "average" child at a rate appropriate for the "average" child.

Many of the plans for enrichment used singly or in combination can be of help in meeting the needs of the bright youngster, especially when the activities or experiences have been planned to provide both breadth and depth in learning. However, these provisions are of the "add-onto" variety and really do not touch the source of the problem.

In terms of these three types of adaptations, a selection of the best features of each used in a carefully planned and integrated program would be far superior to the exclusive use of any one. However, even this would result in a superficial attempt to patch an inadequate and inappropriate program.

Recommended Organization

In recommending an organizational structure for the gifted, it is impossible to separate one skill area and plan for it alone. The total program must be considered and then plans developed for specific sections as parts of a unified whole.

Provision should be made for the early admission of those youngsters who are capable of making adjustment socially, emotionally and academically. Many gifted children will have attended pre-schools and will possess the types of skills and concepts generally presented in kindergarten. Therefore, based on the abilities of each individual it could be beneficial for some children to bypass kindergarten and be placed directly in the primary unit or first grade.

The continuous progress structure appears to have positive qualities for all children through the removal of stigma attached to learning pace, whether slower or faster than the average. This arrangement allows for the integration of abilities and, to some extent, chronological ages. Primary units and intermediate units could reduce the chronological age spans in a group when considered desirable.

Some plan of individualized instruction is recommended especially for skill areas of the curriculum. Diagnosed needs should form the basis for learning prescriptions. Good use can be made of flexible groupings as well as of independent work. The learning pace is set with teacher guidance by each individual to fit his needs and interests. A youngster may choose the size of the learning steps to take and the rate at which to take them. Some children may demonstrate proficiency in the basic requirements in less than the expected average time; they could then move into the next unit if all other factors indicate adjustment. Other gifted youngsters may break the fast forward pace by delving more deeply into special interests. A great amount of flexibility is possible through combining the continuous progress organization with the individualized approach.

The suggested organizational structure and approach are facilitative devices and cannot be fully effective without further measures. A curriculum planned for the average child in a typical graded structure is completely unsuitable for the gifted child. Curriculum revision must include provision for breadth and depth in learning experiences, flexibility and individual needs and interests. No learning design for the gifted can be really beneficial without complete curricular revision.

Class size is another factor to be considered; individualization of learning cannot be employed even adequately when a teacher must work with large numbers of children. Smaller class sizes enable teachers to give each child the individual consideration he needs.

A further requirement is that a sufficient supply of effective multi-media learning materials be readily available. The library must include a large and well-balanced book and periodical collection of good quality, as well as serving as a learning resource center. Full library use from his first year in school through his last year is essential for the gifted youngster.

A crucial ingredient in the success of any program for the gifted is the selection of an excellent teacher.

Teachers of the Gifted

It is hoped that teachers for all children will be the best possible but because of personality, temperament, interest and background some people will be more suited than others to work with very bright young people.

Based on experience and observation, the following traits have been deemed desirable in a teacher of the gifted:

1. GIFTED. At least minimal giftedness is necessary. Teaching the gifted requires a person who has experienced similar needs and interests in order to have real understanding and empathy. The attribute of giftedness is an aid in the building of security and self-confidence. A secure and self-confident teacher is able to accept a child's superior knowledge in a field and encourage him to soar to even greater heights.

2. IMAGINATION AND CURIOSITY. A person must have these qualities in order to be able to recognize, appreciate and encourage them in others. Nothing can be more provoking to one who does not question than an unending stream of questions about everything, many of which require study or research.

3. SUPERIOR EDUCATION. A teacher of the gifted needs a broad academic education as well as outstanding professional preparation. It is important for the teacher to understand basic principles of learning, essential skills and their development, and to be proficient in putting them into practice through a variety of teaching strategies. He must be able to translate the curriculum to fit the particular unique needs of each of the students. The teacher should serve in such capacities as facilitator, question-poser, stimulator, guide, and occasional leader.

4. CAPACITY TO ORGANIZE AND PLAN. A well-organized and functioning room and program contribute to a positive learning environment. Thorough planning based on valid objectives is necessary for comprehensive and balanced learning experiences. Flexibility and the pursuit of special interests need not be restricted by thorough planning.

5. SENSE OF HUMOR. It is important for a child, especially one of high intelligence, to associate with an adult who has a sense of humor and can laugh at himself as well as with others. Humor should be encouraged in bright youngsters since this often is considered to be a necessary quality of a healthy personality.

6. HUMANISM. A truly humanistic teacher is one who demon-

strates through his actions that he respects and prizes each individual for himself, his uniqueness, his ideas, his contributions, and his potential.

The true strength of any program for the gifted resides in the skill, ability and attitudes of the teacher.

Summary

The organization structures of schools are in vertical and horizontal patterns. Vertical refers to the arrangements made for the forward progress of a child during his school years while horizontal describes the adaptations made within a grade or level. Provisions for the gifted have been attempted through modifications of basic vertical and horizontal patterns. These provisions are made through special grouping, acceleration and enrichment. The success of each depends on where, how and with whom it is used. The continuous progress organization which utilizes a plan for individualization of instruction is recommended if it also entails curricular revision, adequate materials, small class size and a carefully selected, excellent teacher.

CHAPTER IV

TEACHING STRATEGIES

Interest and skill in reading usually are typical of the gifted child. These youngsters tend to read more and in a wider variety of areas than the average child. Children with superior ability also have the capacity to put more into their reading and thus to get more out of it. However, without guidance and a planned program, maximal growth rarely will occur. Study has shown that the gifted often read below their mental age potential.

In planning a reading program for the gifted, it is first necessary to identify the expected goals. The following are offered as examples. A reading program for the gifted would be expected to result in:

1. reading fluency achieved through the mastery of applying decoding skills;
2. highly developed comprehension skills which provide for deeper insight and greater awareness of subtleties and nuances of meaning as well as a greater depth and breadth of knowledge in content and interest areas;
3. the skill to evaluate reading matter in terms of authenticity, validity, and objectivity before forming an opinion or determining its usability;
4. the ability to differentiate between good and mediocre literature in terms of literary criteria and to display a pronounced preference for the better literature;
5. the skill to efficiently and effectively compile and organize information from a variety of sources and the ability to locate materials on topics of particular interest;
6. an increased awareness of and the ability to do creative thinking fostered through creative reading;
7. the recognition and use of reading as a source of enjoyment.

In terms of general goals these are not different from those set for every child. The distinctions are in the depth of understanding sought, the experiences and activities used, the materials and teaching methods employed, and the rate for which learning is planned and achieved.

Individualized vs. Basal Reading Approach

It should be noted that the general effectiveness of any reading program is dependent upon its interpretation and use. However, a basal reading program is less effective with youngsters of superior ability because of the content and vocabulary control exercised and the usually strict adherence to restricting vertical sequence progression to grade levels. The vocabulary and content control limits the opportunities in a reading program for learning up to potential, for creating intrinsic motivation and, especially at the primary levels, for experience with good literature. The attribute of being a rapid learner receives little recognition in the rigid enforcement of the grade level sequence structure of the basal reading program. One strength of basal reading plans in terms of the gifted child is the word recognition skills program. Most series are thoroughly planned and sequenced and could provide an excellent resource for implementing diagnostic competency-based instruction.

As an overall plan for achieving the goals identified for a youngster of superior ability, the structure of an individualized approach furnishes ideal possibilities. The characteristics of such a program make it a highly appropriate vehicle for the gifted in acquiring reading skills.

1. Reading material is selected by each pupil with teacher guidance from a wide variety of trade books. This is a contributing factor for intrinsic motivation since the interests and likes of the youngster are the basis for selection.

2. Material selected for reading may be more closely related to the ability of the student either through abstract ideas or through more difficult vocabulary and concepts.

3. The necessary reading skills, word recognition, comprehension, critical reading and study skills are taught through a

systematic program based on diagnosis. Individual or group instruction may be used depending on which is more effective and efficient.

4. The pupil-teacher conference provides the teacher with the opportunity for checking and prescribing basic skill needs, extending critical and creative reading, encouraging learning efforts and building a good rapport.

5. Each child is able to progress at his own rate of learning; he is not held back by others. This progress may be in terms of a combination plan to provide learning in both breadth and depth.

Though an individualized reading program must be carefully planned and organized within a well-defined structure, in operation it lends itself to flexibility, informal arrangements and greater freedom in learning. This is particularly true for gifted children.

General Procedures

There are a variety of general practices that can add to the effectiveness of any curriculum for the gifted. These youngsters are capable of and should be assuming some responsibility for their own learning. The extent of involvement will increase as the child gets older and becomes more experienced. Young children may be included initially in teacher explanations of the purposes of certain methods or practices as well as the reason for learning a specific skill. This idea should be extended throughout the school years. Gradually, the gifted pupil should be included in making both general and specific plans for his own learning. The following example demonstrates implementation of these ideas:

> In looking at the diagnosed skills checklist for Susie, she and her teacher found that mastery of several comprehension skills was lacking. The reasons for developing these skills were discussed and a rank order for study purposes was established. The first skill to be studied was discussed briefly as to its importance and function in the total act of comprehension. Then, Susie and her teacher outlined a specific learning plan including the procedures and materials selected by Susie from available alternatives.

Learning procedures and experiences must never be limited to only one or two possibilities. Instead, there should be a wide variety of alternatives available in order to provide for the individual learning modes of each child. Research has shown that there is no one best way to teach or to learn.

Activity should characterize the learning experiences for gifted children as typified by situations that call for gathering information from a variety of sources, using the total community as a resource and experimenting with or testing hypotheses.

Education for academically talented youngsters requires concentration on developing the understanding and application of concepts, the discussion of ideas and the ability to do critical and creative thinking. The learning of facts should be minimal and restricted only to those areas in which knowledge of facts has been proven to be essential. In reading, emphasis is placed on the application of principles, not the memorization of rules. In other words, it is more important to apply a decoding skill than to state the rule for it.

The mastery of skills is attained through meaningful practice, usually less practice than required by the average child. For the rapid learner, higher standards should be reached in less time than expected of the average child.

Gifted pupils should be encouraged to be imaginative with many assignments providing for originality in completion.

Self-evaluation by gifted youngsters should be encouraged. From the beginning of their school experience, and commensurate with their ability, bright children should learn techniques for self-evaluation.

In any discussion of practices employed with gifted, at least a brief reference must be included pertaining to two basic teaching approaches: those strategies which utilize the inductive and analytical procedures and those which make use of the deductive and synthetic methods. Strategies employing both forms, each where most effective, need to be used with children. Further, it is important that academically superior pupils be given many experiences in which they are required to use both inductive and deductive thinking. More emphasis, however, should be placed on the inductive processes.

Inductive and analytical procedures require reasoning from the particular to the general. This is directly related to divergent thinking which can foster creativity. An example of the utilization of this process is shown by the following:

> The word untie has been given as an example of the prefix "un" with a root word. The meaning of the root word (tie) is compared to the meaning of the derived word (untie). Other root words are used with the prefix "un" to test the meaning implications. Further discussion could lead to other prefixes which produce the negative (not, against) meaning.

Deductive and synthetic approaches as well as convergent thinking involve the process of moving from the general to the particular. Using the preceding example of negative meaning prefixes, the lesson would begin with the generalization that some prefixes change the meaning of a root word from positive to negative. The pupil would be expected to supply specific examples of such prefixes.

Word Recognition Skills

Word recognition skills are taught as means of increasing fluency in the skill of reading. Since reading is a major tool for a gifted child, mastery of skills which foster fluency is essential. However, the preceding general statement is open to a variety of interpretations. The following list sets forth the basic structure for a recommended program:

1. The type and extent of skill proficiency is different with each pupil.
2. Diagnostic procedures for determining attainments and needs are necessary. Examples of questions for checking word recognition skills in the teacher-pupil conference may be found in the book by Spache and Spache.[1]
3. Diagnosis is dependent upon a well-planned and organized skills program.
4. As part of this program, recording devices—perhaps checklists—are needed to provide current data on the specific

---

[1] George D. Spache and Evelyn B. Spache, *Reading in the Elementary School,* 3rd Ed. (Boston, Allyn and Bacon, Inc., 1973), pp. 352–353.

needs of each child. These records should provide for horizontal and vertical progress and move through school with the child.

5. Skills in which competency is shown should be recorded and not formally taught.
6. For those word recognition skills which have been diagnosed as needing direct instruction:
    a. presentation methods and materials must be selected to fit the learning mode of each child;
    b. practice experiences are more effective if integrated into meaningful situations where need is obvious;
    c. direct teaching activities should end immediately upon mastery.
7. Movement in acquiring proficiency in word recognition skills should be fairly rapid and paced to the individual learning rate of each pupil.

Teaching Strategies

Three basic content areas comprise the total structure referred to as word recognition skills. The first deals with sight word development; the study of phonics elements is the second area. Structural analysis is the title of the third content section.

Strategy approaches are discussed briefly within each division. These ideas are simply suggestions which may be modified and extended or used merely as a base for individual creative expression.

Sight Word Development. With gifted children, the main period for building sight words is prior to and along with beginning reading instruction. Possession of a large sight vocabulary speeds the actual act of reading which serves as a stimulus for further activity to produce greater fluency.

The language experience approach was discussed in Chapter II. Its value as a strategy for beginning readers was noted as well as ideas for motivating the experience stories. The following story dictated by a four year old is offered as an example of the vocabulary and concept level that young children may possess. Comparisons may be drawn between the selection and the usual fare offered by preprimers and primers.

The Children Visit the Zoo

The bus driver brings the children to the zoo to see the lonesome Teddy Bear. Someone is waiting for the children in the bus to come. They had to stop at a stop sign. When they got to the zoo they got each of the children some toys. The zoo keeper let the bus driver and the children in.

A bug visited the zoo with the kids. The children walked in the zoo and finally found the zebra. The bus driver drove his bus back to his home and he had to stop again at the stop sign.

The children got tired and had a glass of Pepsi.

The End

It would appear that greater possibilities for growth in beginning reading for gifted pupils reside in the language experience approach than in the basal reading program. Besides serving as an excellent source for sight word learning, this strategy lends itself very well in the reading phase as a means also for teaching the other two areas of word recognition.

Depending on the situation and purpose, groups may be formed to compose experience charts about a particular shared activity. The re-reading of group or individual compositions could include activities similar to the following.

1. "Look at the first sentence, are there any words that you do not know?" Depending on the word, it may be told to the child, it may have some phonic attention called to it or contextual elements may be used in conjunction with phonic skills.
2. "Could you find the word, _____? Frame it with your fingers, please."
3. "Draw a line under the word that tells you how _____. What is the word?"
4. "How many words can you find that begin with the same sound as _____? Could you point to each word and tell us what it is?"
5. "Can you find and draw circles around two words that are pattern (rhyming) words with _____? Can you tell us what these words are?"
6. "Could you find the word that means the same as _____? Point to it and tell us what it is."

7. "Would you read the whole story to yourself? If there are any words you do not know, you may ask me."
8. "Read the story out loud, please."
9. If difficulty is shown with any word, the child should receive added individual help with it after the reading has been completed. Also, he could have a card showing the word made for his own vocabulary file for review purposes.

A strategy beneficial to aiding sight vocabulary growth is the development of skill in using context clues. Instruction in this should begin in initial reading work and continue with refinements added throughout the years until mastery is gained. Some words such as "tear" must be in context in order to be pronounced correctly. This skill is tied directly to the building of comprehension.

An aid to building a sight vocabulary is through the development of a file for each child. This file contains words printed on separate cards which the child has had difficulty recognizing. These cards could be used for individual review by the child or in game situations with other children or with the teacher. As an added feature, synonyms and even antonyms could be elicited and then listed in columns on the back of the card.

A few sample game and drill activities are suggested:
1. Two or more children could identify words from their own set of cards as another player holds up individual cards. The one who has collected the most cards through identification wins.
2. A word bingo game could be constructed based on words from several card files.
3. By putting several cards from his set in order, a child could make phrases that tell where _____ how _____ when _____ etc. He could compete with himself by striving to increase the number of phrases he can make.
4. The cards may be used simply as flashcards with the child identifying as many words as he can in a specified period of time, such as two minutes. Again, this is a way for him to compete with himself.

If considered necessary, standard basic word lists could be used meaningfully with gifted children. The proficiency of the pupil in recognizing the words listed could be checked and those words requiring additional practice could be added to the card file.

Picture dictionaries are useful in helping the child acquire sight vocabulary independently. Selected ABC and counting books also extend sight word acquisition in an enjoyable manner. Listening to a record or tape of the story while reading the book is another resource for learning new words.

PHONICS. The content for instruction in phonics according to Durkin [2] may be described in general terms as letter-sound associations, factors affecting sounds and syllabication. For further descriptions and examples of these areas, it is recommended that the reader consult one or several excellent volumes which deal thoroughly with the topic of phonics.

Although our English-speaking alphabet contains twenty-six letters, descriptive linguists tell us these letters actually represent thirty-three sounds. As described by Holt,[3] these sounds are comprised of twenty-one consonant phonemes, nine simple vowel phonemes, and three semi-vowel phonemes. Although variation does occur, a high percentage (approximately 86% [4]) of phoneme-grapheme regularity exists. Obviously phonics is a valuable tool in the teaching of reading as long as it is treated as one aspect of word recognition and not the whole program.

Academically gifted pupils generally have internalized their own decoding system and require less instruction in this area. When diagnosed needs are found, direct teaching of skills should occur and practice prescribed only until mastery is achieved.

In teaching phonic skills the inductive approach is recommended since generalizations have more meaning for a child when he is able to discover them. Because these generalizations are not always applicable, other skills must be taught. In attacking an unknown word, the child needs to be adept in using a combination of skills.

[2] Dolores Durkin, *Teaching Young Children to Read* (Boston, Allyn and Bacon, Inc., 1972), p. 311.

[3] Charles Lloyd Holt, "A Linguistic Approach to Reading," in Robert E. Chasnoff, ed., *Elementary Curriculum* (New York, Pitman Publishing Corp., 1964), p. 253.

[4] Donald C. Cushenbery, *Reading Improvement in The Elementary School* (West Nyack, Parker Publishing Co., Inc., 1969), p. 71.

Because of their learning ability and usually advanced skill attainment, gifted children in the upper elementary levels gain added perception about their language through use of several of the basic linguistic findings. Regularity in spelling-sound patterns could be given attention, such as the common CVC, CVCe and CVVC patterns. Some gifted youngsters respond with great interest in reading and learning about the history of the English language and the structural and phonic changes which have occurred. The book by the Epsteins,[5] *The First Book of Words —Their Family Histories,* is very readable and a good introduction to this topic. Related to this, Gold [6] has recommended that gifted children be exposed to one of the more sophisticated forms of word attack which is the ". . . recognition of words by their derivation from other languages."

STRUCTURAL ANALYSIS. A child may find additional clues to word recognition through an understanding of the principles concerning word structure. In fact, a child should be taught to study the structure of an unfamiliar word before considering the sound elements. Basically, structural analysis deals with derived words, those which have affixes added, and inflected words, those which change due to grammatical usage. Compound words could reasonably be included in this area. Where these are found in context, generally attention need only be called to their structural form.

Inflected words, particularly plurals, should be the formal introduction to structural analysis; these could be followed fairly rapidly with —ed and —ing endings. Most gifted children will need little more instruction with these simpler forms and endings than having such changes and their meanings called to their attention. An inductive approach again is recommended.

Derived words are root words combined with affixes (prefixes and suffixes). Generally, it is a sound practice to begin with prefixes plus roots before moving to roots plus suffixes. Rapid learners will absorb this quickly and with guidance of an inductive nature they will be able to deduce fine shades of meaning and

[5] Sam Epstein and Beryl Epstein, *The First Book of Words—Their Family Histories* (New York, Franklin Watts, Inc., 1954).

[6] Milton J. Gold, *Education of The Intellectually Gifted* (Columbus, Charles E. Merrill Books, Inc., 1965), p. 210.

relationships of affixes. Barbe [7] has compiled an extensive list of affixes as well as a list of common Latin roots which teachers and gifted pupils will find useful and interesting.

As well as learning the meanings of affixes and how an affix affects a particular root, it is necessary that a pupil can pronounce the new word and understand its syllabication.

Further word power, as well as interest, could be gained by integrating the teaching of synonyms and antonyms with suffixes and prefixes and then studying the relationships of changes in word meanings.

Comprehension Skills

In terms of education for the gifted, mere competence in the basic comprehension skills is insufficient. If the full potential of these youngsters is to be developed, reading comprehension must be utilized to the greatest depths. For example, there is quite a difference in merely feeling satisfied when the tiger is changed back into a mouse at the end of the fable *Once a Mouse* [8] and in contemplating with the hermit the total implications—not just the physical connotations—of the words big and little. Comprehension is more than the reception of ideas; it involves reacting to them by invoking thought processes to produce more ideas and more complex understandings of ideas.

There is no overall sequential order in the acquisition of comprehension skills; instead consideration must be given to the various aspects from the very beginning of reading instruction. Even the young gifted child is able and ready to go beyond the literal comprehension stage.

Teaching Strategies

The skill areas involved in producing reading comprehension as well as general strategy suggestions are summarized in this section.

RELEVANT DETAILS. There are numerous times when it is

[7] Walter B. Barbe, *Educator's Guide to Personalized Reading Instruction* (Englewood Cliffs, Prentice-Hall, Inc., 1961), pp. 196–200.

[8] Marcia Brown, *Once a Mouse* (New York, Charles Scribner's Sons, 1961).

necessary to read for specific details; therefore, the rapid learner should have instruction in developing this skill. Under no circumstances does this refer to the type of inane questions usually asked and exemplified by the following: "Who was playing with the dog?" "What was the dog's name?" "What did mother want Billy to do?"

The following points are suggested for consideration in teaching youngsters to find relevant details:

1. Material most appropriate to reading for detail should be used. Material could cover areas of science, social studies, identification factors or recipes. Fiction stories seldom require this type of detailed reading.
2. The specific purpose or purposes for which the reading is being done should be discussed and set.
3. Details selected should be checked for relevancy against the set purpose. Items not pertinent should be discussed briefly to determine specifically why they are inappropriate and perhaps for what purposes or circumstances they may have been relevant.
4. Skimming and scanning skills require direct teaching. Their use must be understood for efficiency in locating detailed information.
5. After the information has been located, it should be pointed out that a thorough and slower reading approach is needed to select and absorb details.

Main Idea. For gifted youngsters, instruction in finding main ideas should employ experiences using paragraphs, sections and complete works from both fiction and non-fiction material. For real depth, emphasis should be placed on capturing the thought process of the author by reading the entire piece to draw the basic idea from the whole and not just from a single topic sentence. The search for one sentence may tend to interfere with or restrict the possibilities for full understanding.

Referring again to the fable, *Once a Mouse*,[9] children easily understand that the tiger deserved to be changed back into a mouse because he was planning to kill his benefactor. This is only

[9] *Ibid.*

a surface level of comprehension, and the teacher must not allow the gifted pupil to stop at this point. Further discussion might include ideas as:

"What other solutions besides changing the tiger back into a mouse could have been used by the hermit?"

"If other options were open to him, why did the hermit change the tiger back into a mouse?"

"What do you think was meant by the last sentence?"

"What do the words big and little mean?"

"Can you think of several meanings for these words?"

"What meaning do you think they have in this fable?"

SUMMARIZING. The ability to summarize material that has been read aids comprehension in that it forces a reader to follow the structure of a selection or the development of a plot by finding the main points and their explanatory details.

Summarizing also requires that attention be given to sequences. A variety of sequence types can be found in written works:

1. chronological;
2. procedural;
3. cause-effect;
4. ideational—ideas building on one another;
5. levels of difficulty.

Determining the sequence used in a piece of writing reveals the relationships involved and increases the ability of the student to summarize or remember the material.

1. Students may be asked to give a very brief summary of a trade book they have enjoyed to arouse interest in others to read the book. Guidance in planning the summary is necessary.
2. Brief summaries of trade books could be written on cards to be filed and used by all pupils when help is desired in selecting a book.
3. Planning for presenting a story through creative drama necessitates identifying the main parts and sequence of the material in order to carry out the drama.
4. In the pupil-teacher conference, the student could be asked to give a one or two sentence summary of the book he has read.

5. A child could write a summary in the style of a telegram message.
6. Establishing a chronological or cause-effect sequence in relation to an event or circumstance in history or the broader area of social studies—i.e., the events leading to the Civil War or factors involved in the location of cities—will help in understanding the material.
7. The importance of finding and following a procedural sequence could be demonstrated through performing science experiments.

PARALANGUAGE AND SYNTACTICAL CLUES. The term paralanguage refers to stress, pitch and juncture in speaking and reading. Because paralanguage is basic to comprehension it is learned and applied usually through the process of imitation. Gifted children in elementary grades can profit through greater facility with language by understanding the distinctions and changes possible through control of stress, pitch and juncture.

Juncture, the pauses between morphemic elements or ideas, is signaled by punctuation marks and spaces between words. Examples will aid students in noticing the changes in meaning when punctuation is expressed.

Let's race Bill. Let's race, Bill.
Let's race Bill? Let's race Bill!

Although stress and pitch commonly find expression in oral reading or language, they may also be applied subconsciously to discern an unclear shade of meaning.

Children could be asked to apply stress to each underlined word and note the refinements in meaning.

She plays well. She plays well. She plays well.

The numbers 1–4 above morphemes indicate the pitch level with 4 usually designated as the highest pitch. The number 2 is the arbitrary starting level with 3 indicating a slightly higher pitch and 1 a slightly lower pitch. The extreme level is shown by a 4 and is rarely used. An indicated level is sustained until a new level is marked. The ↑ appearing at the end of the sentence also means that the last level has been maintained.

²Are you ³jok′ing³↑?

The concept that the three elements of paralanguage function together should be made clear to pupils.

Syntactical clues are those found in the arrangement of words, sentences and paragraphs. Consider the meaning implications with the change in placement of just one word.

> He ran also.
> He also ran.

A recognition by gifted pupils of the possibilities inherent in paralanguage and syntactical clues will add new dimensions to their comprehension abilities.

INFERENCE AND PREDICTION. The ability to use the skills of inference and prediction denotes advanced levels of reading comprehension. Use of these skills demands that the pupil be actively involved in reading by searching beyond what the writer says to what he means.

Inferential reading requires the student to use the printed page as the source for thought to achieve depth in understanding through defining the purpose of the author, through forming generalizations and conclusions and through perceiving implied relationships. These same understandings can also be utilized by the learner in predicting outcomes.

Guidance in the development of these skills should be given from the beginning of reading instruction and advance to keener perceptions as rapidly as warranted by the learning ability of the individual.

In most instances, the reading conference will provide the best setting for instruction in inference and prediction for the rapid learner.

One strategy would have the child read several paragraphs from a given selection but before reaching the climax, questions, as the following, could be used in a discussion.

"What kind of person do you think _____ is? Why do you think so?"

"How does he feel about _____? What makes you think this?"

"What will he do about _____? Why do you think he would follow this course of action?"

The pupil should finish reading the story and in the follow-up discussion a comparison made of the predicted outcome with the written one.

Further questions could explore the intent or purpose of the author in writing the story, as: "What idea did the story try to convey?" or "Why do you think the author wrote the story?"

STYLE DEVICES. Gifted pupils in the elementary school have the ability to gain a deeper and richer understanding of what they read through recognition and study of literary style devices. Use is made in trade books even for young children of such writing techniques as metaphors, analogies, allegories, sarcasm, subtlety and satire.

Consider the metaphors in Mary O'Neill's book, *Hailstones and Halibut Bones* [10] in which colors are compared to and described as emotions, objects, smells, actions, etc. Cyrano de Bergerac [11] uses metaphors in the humorous but poignant description of his nose as he points out the lack of imagination and wit used by the man who has insulted him. These word pictures elicit imagination, emotion and contemplation from the reader.

Without recognizing the form and understanding the intent of satire, the subtlety and humor as well as the meaning of the story is lost in a book such as *The Pushcart War* by Jean Merrill. [12]

Study of such devices not only adds depth and fullness to the comprehension ability of a pupil, it also affords him enrichment in his own use of language.

Critical Reading Skills

Critical reading is reading beyond the level of comprehension; it requires that the reader evaluate the material in terms of truth, authority and value to fit his own purposes. In order to do this, the reader must have received direct teaching in the skills in-

[10] Mary O'Neill, *Hailstones and Halibut Bones* (Garden City, Doubleday and Company, Inc., 1961).

[11] Edmond Rostand, *Cyrano de Bergerac* (Garden City, Doubleday, Page and Co., 1898), Act First.

[12] Jean Merrill, *The Pushcart War* (New York, William R. Scott, Inc., 1964).

volved. Although curiosity and intellectual and reading maturity may have led a gifted child to develop some critical reading skills, instruction must be provided to sharpen these skills and develop additional abilities.

The reader must determine:

1. the competency of the author to write on such a subject and his possible biases;
2. whether opinion or fact has been presented and if all of the facts, not just selected ones, are included;
3. whether the conclusions reached are logical as indicated by the evidence.

The teaching of critical reading is not meant to produce negativism. Instead, it is designed to develop a discerning and intelligent reader who will consider all facets of what he reads.

Teaching Strategies

1. After a statement of fact from a written selection has been elicited from the pupil, the teacher could open a discussion by asking for proof of the fact. The offered proof could lead into a study of the authority or qualifications of the writer. Discussion could deal also with the intent or background of the author and how this could affect objectivity and create bias. Possible commitments of the publisher also merit scrutiny.
2. By using a variety of selections, comparisons could be made of points based on fact and those based on opinion. Activities could include:
   a. checking for cited evidence or references;
   b. consulting other sources;
   c. studying original sources.
3. Since a basically factual account of an incident or situation may be subtly slanted through the effective selection and use of words and phrases, gifted children should be taught to recognize and understand the use of emotion-laden words in differentiating opinion from fact. A rapid learner may find enjoyment and enlightenment in the consideration of materials as demonstrated by the following familiar cliché in its original and rewritten forms:

The early bird catches the worm.

The bird arrived at dawn to prepare his cowardly ambush for the hapless worm.

It must also be shown that the use of color and feeling words is necessary in fictional materials and in some nonfiction writing.

4. In the pupil-teacher conference, the conclusion reached in an article could be identified and checked against the main points to determine if it is logical or faulty. This process could be reversed somewhat by having the learner write a conclusion from the list of facts presented, then compare it to the original conclusion.

Creative Reading Skills

For gifted pupils, the development of creative reading skills must be considered a necessary part of the regular program of reading instruction. These skills should receive attention at the earliest levels of formal schooling.

Creative reading may be described as a process in which the printed page serves as the source for imaginative and original thought production by the reader. Creative reading and creative thinking are so closely related they are practically synonymous. Reading often serves as the impetus for research discoveries and inventions.

The entire creative process can be fostered by a teacher who accepts and lives the premise that there is no one way to do anything. A teacher must encourage the production of creative ideas and recognize that occasional time for daydreaming or looking out the window could be a period of incubation.

Teaching Strategies

The following are examples of possible teaching ideas:

1. After reading part of the story, the child may be asked to supply an ending for it or several possibilities for endings.
2. Characterization clues could provide sources for suppositions of behavior patterns in hypothetical situations.
3. Historical matter provides a great wealth of material to prompt creative thinking. An example: "If George Wash-

ington had continued in the profession of surveying, what historical differences, if any, do you think this would have made?"

4. Divergent thinking is called for with questions based on reading content such as the following: "In what other ways could you use _____?" "Is that the only way that _____ could have solved the problem? What would you have done instead?"
"How do you think that _____ will do _____?"

5. After studying and reading mythology, a child could be asked to tell or write his explanation in mythological style of something in his environment.

Study Skills

Proficiency in study skills is required for in-depth research and critical reading and thinking activities engaged in by gifted students. As well as the usual topics included in the study skills, gifted pupils should receive instruction as early as possible and according to need in the use of: the card catalog, cross references, periodical guides, charts, graphs, tables, maps, timetables, atlases and other reference materials. Further skills include:

1. learning how to select the appropriate and best sources for the topic under study;
2. how to take effective notes from written and oral material efficiently;
3. how to organize these notes;
4. how to make an outline of the materials gathered. Different types of techniques for reporting should be taught and competence developed in using them. Study skills as well as reporting methods are taught more profitably through a practical application approach.

Summary

General goals for reading instruction for the rapid learner must be developed and a program planned to achieve these objectives. An individualized approach based on the use of trade books is preferred to a basal reading program for academically superior children. Reading instruction for these pupils should be based upon a diagnostic approach in which basic skills are taught when specific needs are shown with pacing dependent upon the rapid learning rate of the child. This is recommended particularly for word recognition skills and basic comprehension skills.

Gifted children should be guided to achieve greater depth and perception in comprehension than the average child. Because these youngsters have superior academic ability and wide-reaching interests, an understanding of and proficiency in the skills of critical reading are required. This is fostered by an inquiring and truth-seeking attitude. The full potential of the gifted pupil will not be reached without development of creative reading and thinking. Because of their need to be engaged in depth research and critical reading and thinking, it is urgent that these children receive early instruction in all of the study skills.

CHAPTER V

ENRICHMENT

F OR THE GIFTED, enrichment is not the average curriculum fare with special activities or projects added. An enriched curriculum must be planned as the regular program for these youngsters. The experiences chosen must challenge students while developing necessary concepts and skills. In devising a special curriculum for gifted students, it would be wise for any system to develop criteria for the selection of materials and experiences to be included.

No attempt has been made in this chapter to establish a curriculum for the gifted. The purpose instead is to suggest types of activities and experiences that will make the reading program worthwhile for these children.

Learning Activities

These ideas include both individual and group activities which attempt to deepen comprehension, broaden vocabulary and stimulate critical and creative thinking. For the purpose of general guidance, level placement sections were used; however, in no way are these meant to be prescriptive. Many variations of these levels will and should occur.

Early Primary

It is essential to acquaint academically bright youngsters on the pre-school, kindergarten and first grade levels with a variety of good literature, both by reading to them and in their own reading selections.

Folk Stories. Besides being enjoyable, many of these stories are excellent to use in building ideas of simple plot development and structure to aid comprehension.

1. An understanding of simple plot structure may be devel-

oped from stories such as: *The Three Billy Goats Gruff, Jack and the Beanstalk, The Three Little Pigs,* and Wanda Gag's *Millions of Cats.*[1] In each of these, the introduction briefly designates the setting and establishes the problem or goal with a series of episodes leading to the logical climax and a satisfying and quick ending.

Discussion could begin along the lines of: "When did the story take place?" "Where did it take place?" "Who is the main character (characters)?" "What was he (were they) going to do?" "Could you tell where in the story you learned these things?" The term, introduction, and its use could be built at this time. Further discussion would center on plot development, shown through the simple, rather repetitive episodes. "What events happened after the introduction?" If this appears difficult initially, attention should be called to the sequence of events. "What happened first . . . second . . . etc.?" What happened that caused the ending of the story?" "What part told how the story ended?" The other terms describing story parts could be used and defined as they are discussed.

2. Plot structures of these stories can be compared. The following as related by the children could be listed on a chalkboard, chart or transparency. Similarities become very graphic:

The Three Billy Goats Gruff	*The Three Little Pigs*
Introduction:	Introduction:
When: Once upon a time	When: Once upon a time
Where: not told	Where: not told
Who: Three Billy Goats Gruff	Who: Three Little Pigs
Problem: wanted more grass to eat	Problem: must leave home
must cross a bridge guarded by a troll	must provide for themselves
Development:	Development:
First event: littlest Billy Goat crosses	First event: first Little Pig builds home of

[1] Wanda Gag, *Millions of Cats* (New York, Coward-McCann, Inc., 1928).

	the bridge and meets the troll		straw and meets the wolf
Second event:	middle-sized Billy Goat crosses the bridge and meets the troll	Second event:	second Little Pig builds home of sticks and meets the wolf
Third event:	big Billy Goat crosses the bridge and meets the troll	Third event:	third Little Pig builds home of bricks and meets the wolf
Climax:	Big Billy Goat Gruff kills the troll	Climax:	third Little Pig kills the wolf
Ending:	Three Billy Goats Gruff ate their fill	Ending:	Lived happily ever after

Comparisons may be drawn while recording the second story or at the end of it. Children may be asked if they know of other stories with similar plot structures or the teacher might mention several familiar stories and have the children decide which correspond in development.

3. A simple outline similar to the one shown could aid youngsters in building the story sequence for participation in storytelling.

4. While making comparisons of stories as the preceding, gifted youngsters could begin to identify simple themes through questions such as the following: "Did you agree with the climax and ending of the story? Why?" "Was the climax of the story fair? Why?"

5. Children could illustrate the climax of a story by using various art media.

REALISTIC STORIES. Realistic stories prove to be a source of enjoyment for young children because they are stories that deal with the known, the everyday and the commonplace. These as well as folk stories could be viewed in terms of plot structure and development.

1. Examples of stories with relatively basic plot structures but good appeal are: *Evan's Corner* by Elizabeth Starr Hill,[2] *Who Will Be My Friends?* by Syd Hoff,[3] *Peter's Chair* by Ezra Jack Keats,[4] and *What Mary Jo Shared* by Janice Udry.[5] As shown with folk stories, children can be guided to identify the major sections of the story.

2. Similarities and differences of plot development could be drawn between folk stories and realistic stories noting such things as:
   a. similarities in basic plot structure;
   b. differences in specificity of setting;
   c. differences in situations or types of problems posed;
   d. amounts and types of action portrayed.
   In studying such areas, the following ideas could be used:
   a. Set up two stories for comparison in chart form.
   b. A group-made bulletin board could show the contrasts in picture form.
   c. Roll movies of children's illustrations of stories of the two types could be made and used to point out similarities and differences.
   d. Pictures illustrating the climaxes of the two types of stories could be drawn by children and displayed.

3. Identification of the theme should again be given consideration and comparisons drawn between the themes of stories as illustrated by *Evan's Corner* and *Peter's Chair*. In the first, the youngster learns that satisfaction comes not just from possessing one's own corner in a home but in sharing with others in the family. The latter expresses a similar idea that all members of a family can live together and share in all ways with each still occupying a unique position.

POETRY. It is to be hoped that these youngsters will have acquired at an early age a broad and generous background in

[2] Elizabeth Starr Hill, *Evan's Corner* (New York, Holt, Rinehart and Winston, Inc., 1967).

[3] Syd Hoff, *Who Will Be My Friends?* (New York, Harper & Row, Publishers, 1960).

[4] Ezra Jack Keats, *Peter's Chair* (New York, Harper & Row, Publishers, 1967).

[5] Janice Udry, *What Mary Jo Shared* (Chicago, Albert Whitman, 1966).

nursery rhymes. Initially, gifted children should have poetry read to them. Many experiences of hearing poetry read well should be provided; the type of poetry will depend on the likes and interests of the child. Limericks, nonsense rhymes, humorous poetry and narrative poetry are good forms to use with beginners in poetry. In addition, collections of poems such as *Miracles* (collected by Richard Lewis [6]) written by children of similar ages could provide further understanding of poetry and possible stimulation for personal creativity.

1. Simple form and meter could be introduced to gifted children through the guided process of creating a piece such as a limerick or haiku.
2. Rather than focusing on rhyming patterns, the idea of expressing a thought or an emotion effectively should be stressed.
3. Narrative poetry tells a story and is easy to understand. As such, it can serve as an introduction for developing comprehension from works in the poetic form. A short and simple story of the results of teasing is told by Laura E. Richards in "The Monkeys and the Crocodile" while true bravery is shown humorously in "Custard the Dragon" by Ogden Nash.
   a. After hearing either of these poems, literal comprehension could be discussed and the child could be asked to draw a picture of what happened to the fifth monkey or a picture of the character who showed real bravery in the poem, "Custard the Dragon."
   b. With some teacher guidance, gifted children can discover that narrative poetry contains all of the elements in the simple plot structure of a story.
4. Poetry employing nonsense words can be used beneficially with the gifted as a form for language study. After hearing this form of poetry, children could contribute their own nonsense words to a list on a board or chart from which a group poem could be created. An informal discussion utilizing the group-produced poem could lead toward an attempt to categorize the nonsense words as nouns (name words),

[6] Richard Lewis (comp.) *Miracles; Poems by Children of the English-Speaking World* (New York, Simon and Schuster, 1966).

verbs (doing or being words) and adjectives or adverbs (describing words). This type of activity leads into the concept of identifying words through their form and function in a sentence.

CREATIVE DRAMATICS. Besides serving as a stimulus for reading stories and poems, participation in creative dramatics fosters comprehension through study of plot development and characterization.

1. Plot development becomes clear when children and teacher identify the scenes in sequence to be portrayed in the drama.
2. Characterization must be developed through the interpretation given by each child as to how he believes or feels that the character would act or what he would say.
3. The importance of style matching context has strong possibilities for development also, in that children must create their own dialogue to portray a specific character in a story. If the story for the drama is from traditional or folk literature, the teacher could demonstrate dialogue appropriate in the folk setting contrasted to dialogue of the contemporary period and let children make observations and draw conclusions.

VOCABULARY DEVELOPMENT. Even some gifted youngsters will be lacking an adequate language background to start reading. Chapter II dealt with ideas for building background through varied experiences. Simple alphabet books read to youngsters or used individually by pupils help build a sight vocabulary. Examples of such books are: *The Alphabet Tale* by Jan Garten,[7] *Brian Wildsmith's ABC*,[8] *Bruno Munari's ABC*,[9] *Celestino Piatti's Animal ABC*,[10] *Ape in a Cape* by Fritz Eichenberg[11] and *A for the Ark* by Roger Duvoisin.[12] After some experience

---

[7] Jan Garten, *The Alphabet Tale* (New York, Random House, 1964).

[8] Brian Wildsmith, *Brian Wildsmith's ABC* (New York, Franklin Watts, 1963)

[9] Bruno Munari, *Bruno Munari's ABC* (Cleveland, World Publishing Co., 1960).

[10] Celestino Piatti, *Celestino Piatti's Animal ABC* (New York, Atheneum, 1966).

[11] Fritz Eichenberg, *Ape in a Cape* (New York, Harcourt, Brace & World, 1952).

[12] Roger Duvoisin, *A for the Ark* (New York, Lothrop, Lee, and Shepard, 1952).

with these books, a child could make his own alphabet book.

For gifted children already reading, advanced alphabet books can be fun as well as an aid to increasing word power. *I Love My Anteater With an A* by Dahlov Ipcar [13] is a good example of alliteration besides providing experiences with unusual words and humorous ideas.

Middle Elementary

Work begun at the lower levels should continue, with increased depth planned for and expected from youngsters typically placed in second through fourth grade levels.

FOLK STORIES. The various forms of traditional literature afford enjoyment, reading practice, examples of several literary forms and a variety of levels of comprehension.

1. The basic motifs found in folk tales are easy to identify and use to increase comprehension. Further understanding may be gained by writing parallel stories using motif patterns. After reading different versions of a tale, cultural influences on style could be discussed and comparisons drawn. As an example, the popular Perrault version of *Cinderella* could be compared to the Irish version, *Fair, Brown and Trembling*, or the English version, *Catskin*, or others. Some research skills may be gained in locating different stories.

2. Fables illustrate a different type of style structure related to their didactic purpose. Understanding the form could include delving into the history of the fable and its purpose. Gifted youngsters might enjoy writing their own fables. As a strategy, a list could be compiled of familiar clichés; the pupil would select one and use it as the moral for an original fable accompanied by an illustration of the literal meaning of the cliché. An example might be, "gilding the lily."

3. The purpose and form of fables and parables could be compared.

[13] Dahlov Ipcar, *I Love My Anteater with an A* (New York, Alfred A. Knopf, 1964).

4. The compilation of a directory of American folk heroes, including a map showing the locale of each, would provide opportunities for research, reading skill development and enjoyment.

FICTIONAL STORIES. These stories, whether fantasy, realistic or historical in nature, continue to provide sources for reading enjoyment as well as vicarious experiences, vocabulary building and study.

1. Plot structure more advanced than the simple form of development when studied and understood will add increased depth to understanding. The plot development of parallel events that merge is used in *Blueberries for Sal* by Robert McCloskey.[14] *Strawberry Girl* by Lois Lenski[15] is an example of plot development using episodes which build and flow together for a final climax.

2. Identification of the story theme will give depth in comprehension and increase appreciation of the story.

3. Comparisons of the treatment used in stories with similar themes could be made with books such as *Blue Willow* by Doris Gates[16] and *Roosevelt Grady* by Louise Shotwell,[17] *Crow Boy* by Taro Yashima[18] and *The Hundred Dresses* by Eleanor Estes,[19] or *Macaroon* by Julia Cunningham[20] and *Amigo* by Byrd Schweitzer.[21]

4. Realistic stories also provide excellent sources for characterization study. Comparisons could be drawn between characters in flat dimension and those who show growth and change; for example, *Homer Price*[22] could be compared to the main character in . . . *And Now Miguel*.[23] Be-

[14] Robert McCloskey, *Blueberries for Sal* (New York, The Viking Press, 1948).

[15] Lois Lenski, *Strawberry Girl* (New York, J. B. Lippincott Co., 1945).

[16] Doris Gates, *Blue Willow* (New York, The Viking Press, 1940).

[17] Louise Shotwell, *Roosevelt Grady* (Cleveland, World Publishing Co., 1963).

[18] Taro Yashima, *Crow Boy* (New York, The Viking Press, 1955).

[19] Eleanor Estes, *The Hundred Dresses* (New York, Harcourt, Brace & Jovanovich).

[20] Julia Cunningham, *Macaroon* (New York, Pantheon, 1962).

[21] Byrd Schweitzer, *Amigo* (New York, The Macmillan Co., 1963).

[22] Robert McCloskey, *Homer Price* (New York, The Viking Press, 1943).

[23] Joseph Krumgold, . . . *And Now Miguel* (New York, Thomas Y. Crowell Co., 1953).

cause of their intellectual ability, gifted pupils should be introduced earlier than average youngsters to implicit characterization development. Characterization concepts may be developed through such ideas as:

   a. Questioning—"What are your feelings about _____? Why do you feel that way?"

   b. Predicting—The teacher could suggest different situations and let the child predict how he thinks the character would act in each.

   c. Comparing—Given one implicitly drawn character, the child could point out trait likenesses and differences with another implicitly shown character.

5. The elements in stories leading into fantasy can be identified easily and discussed. Retelling the story using minimal revision to make it realistic could be done by children. Follow-up discussion could point out parts of the story which required change and the type of change needed. Symbolism used in the fantasy should be noted and interpreted. When studying symbolism with youngsters capable of understanding it, introductory discussion would encompass what is meant by symbolism as well as how and why it is used.

6. Comparisons of the treatments of animals as characters could be shown through stories such as:

   a. For younger readers: *Anatole* by Eve Titus,[24] *Make Way for Ducklings* by Robert McCloskey [25] and *The Biggest Bear* by Lynd Ward.[26]

   b. For older readers: *Wind in the Willows* by Kenneth Grahame,[27] *Charlotte's Web* by E. B. White [28] and *Hurry Home, Candy* by Meindert DeJong.[29]

[24] Eve Titus, *Anatole* (New York, Whittlesey House, 1956).

[25] Robert McCloskey, *Make Way for Ducklings* (New York, The Viking Press, 1941).

[26] Lynd Ward, *The Biggest Bear* (Boston, Houghton Mifflin Co., 1952).

[27] Kenneth Grahame, *Wind in the Willows* (New York, Charles Scribner's Sons, 1927).

[28] E. B. White, *Charlotte's Web* (New York, Harper & Row, Publishers, 1952).

[29] Meindert DeJong, *Hurry Home, Candy* (New York, Harper & Brothers Publishers, 1953).

Children could show differences in characterization by illustrating characters from each story through art media, discussion or creative drama. Added understanding could be built through consideration of ideas as the following: Suppose the characterization treatments of animals in *Wind in the Willows* and *Charlotte's Web* were exchanged, what would this do to each story?

7. Research and study skills could be taught and practiced meaningfully through an activity like compiling a book of information about favorite authors and illustrators selected by the class. A variety of language skills including letter writing can be gained from such activities.

POETRY. Interest in and appreciation of poetry should continue to be developed along with understanding it as a literary form. It should be stressed, however, as with all literature, poetry should not be scrutinized and dissected until it is ruined as a source of pleasure.

1. The classical Mother Goose rhymes could be compared to the American versions of Mother Goose in terms of language, content and overall style.

2. Besides enjoying the form, poetry should be studied for meaning to the individual child. Depth should be sought through the background of experience of the child rather than through set analysis procedures.

3. The use of figures of speech is shown effectively in poetry. Similies and metaphors can be identified and their application discussed. "Fog" by Carl Sandburg, "Dandelion" by Hilda Conkling or "O Captain! My Captain!" by Walt Whitman are excellent examples of the metaphor. Similies may be found in poems as: "Hallowe'en" by Henry Behn, "Barter" by Sara Teasdale or "The Star" by Jane Taylor. School and class activities or surroundings may be used as sources for student written phrases or sentences using similies and metaphors.

BOOK DISCUSSIONS. Interested pupils should be given the opportunity to participate in small group discussions of commonly read books. Such an activity may increase the depth of comprehension, broaden the field of perception and activate both critical and creative thinking. A book may be viewed in terms of such areas as literary criteria, social aspects or symbolism.

NEWSPAPERS. Newspapers for children may provide an introduction and transition to the understanding and use of a regular newspaper.

1. Youngsters should be guided to recognize that the content of newspaper articles deals with real people and events of interest to many readers.
2. Children can identify various sections of the newspaper and describe the purpose of each.
3. Assignments can be made for specific items of information commonly found in the newspaper.

VOCABULARY ENRICHMENT ACTIVITIES. During this stage of development, many gifted pupils enjoy learning about words as well as learning new and unusual words.

1. Words such as subject, desert or content may be listed and children asked to pronounce and define them or use them in meaningful sentences. Studying the differences in accent and meaning should point out the concept that single word units may be incomprehensible without a contextual base.
2. Synonyms for designated words in a story could be supplied by a child. Study of the changes in shades of meaning carried by some synonyms should be developed. Antonyms could be studied similarly.
3. Literal and figurative language will often provide humor with learning. The various *Amelia Bedelia*[30] books by Peggy Parish illustrate very entertainingly the literal interpretation of figurative language. Children could make their own booklets of common figurative phrases accompanied by illustrations of the literal meanings.

Upper Elementary

Gifted students in the age range of average fifth and sixth graders may have reading abilities ranging up to and beyond the tested twelfth grade level. Activities must be stimulating

[30] Peggy Parish, *Amelia Bedelia* (New York, Harper & Row, Publishers, 1963).

and challenging while continuing to develop skills in depth and to provide a knowledge of literature in breadth.

MYTHOLOGY. Classical Greek mythology provides students with the opportunity to study the attempts of earlier civilizations to explain their world. It also represents pleasurable reading of stories, some simple, others abstract and complex with symbolism. As well as to Greek mythology, these children should be exposed to the study of mythology from other cultures, such as Norse, Indian, Hawaiian, African and American Indian.

1. Using myths which explain such phenomena as the changing seasons, constellations or spider webs in storytelling provides an easy to understand yet interesting and personal introduction to this form of literature. Children may wish to prepare myths to tell to groups or even other classes.
2. Myths that explain should be presented to students in both the classical form and the more primitive "why" form. These forms could be compared for topic, setting and style.
3. Classical myths could also be compared with Norse myths, African myths and Hawaiian myths. Differences in imagery and symbolism provide bases for discussion.
4. Using the myth style with gods and goddesses, children could write explanations of objects or phenomena in their environment such as: billboards, super highways, smog or subways. These original myths may be used also for creative drama.

EPICS. The accounts of brave men performing daring deeds are enticing stories for readers. Such epics as the "Iliad," the "Odyssey," "Beowulf," "King Arthur," "Sigurd," the "Song of Roland," "Robin Hood" and "Paka'a" from *Backbone of the King* by Marcia Brown [31] are literary experiences recommended for gifted youngsters.

1. Comparisons of time periods and characterizations can be made of epics and their heroes as in Beowulf and King Arthur. The forms of comradeship could be considered as they are shown in Robin Hood and King Arthur.

[31] Marcia Brown, *Backbone of the King* (New York, Charles Scribner's Sons, 1966).

2. The student could identify the morals and values of the time and culture as demonstrated through the hero of the story read. Comparisons of these topics could be drawn among the eras and cultures represented in the various epics.

3. The epic as a literary form and style should receive an appropriate amount of study. For a project, a gifted student could elect to create an epic of a modern man; topics may be similar to the following: "A Commuter's Odyssey," "The Quest for a Golden Harvest" or "The Knights of the Space Station."

MOTHER GOOSE. Though these rhymes are generally associated with younger children, older gifted pupils could gain some insights into life in another age through an introductory study of the speculated origins and meanings of various Mother Goose rhymes. Sources such as *The Annotated Mother Goose* [32] could be used for this type of study. Students could select a contemporary national, state, local or school issue or event and write a rhyme in the Mother Goose style about it. Added understanding of form and effective word usage may be gained from such an activity.

CRITICAL READING. Historical or modern events are excellent media to use in developing critical reading skills.

1. To illustrate the concept that history books are the interpretation by the author of the research he has conducted, various versions of an event or period may be read and compared by the student. For example, materials could be obtained from other countries or regions about topics as: the War of 1812, the United States version and the Canadian version; the American Revolution, our version and the British version; or the Civil War, as viewed by the North and the South.

2. If it is possible to obtain a copy or to view an original document, diary or journal, suggest that a youngster read the material and write his own account of the event or hap-

[32] William and Ceil Baring-Gould, *The Annotated Mother Goose* (New York, Clarkson N. Potter, Inc., 1962).

pening. Interpretative skills and an understanding of how history is written may be increased. A critique of the work should include a careful study of the relevance or factual basis for conclusions drawn or statements made.

3. The teacher working with one or two students could plan and stage a surprise incident before a group of gifted youngsters. Without conversation or discussion, each child would be instructed to write his version of what happened and perhaps why it occurred. Sharing and comparing the completed accounts will illustrate that people may view and record the same event in different ways. In-depth analysis by each student of his own background, experiences, biases and objectives may lead to generalizations about reasons for possible differences in the versions.

PRINTED NEWS MEDIA. A more intensive study of the newspaper and other printed news sources should be included in a program for the gifted.

1. Children could study the structure of the news article and then compare it to the typical story structure.
2. The style of writing used in news articles could be studied and compared to different writing techniques used in fictional stories.
3. A study of the editorial section including editorial cartoons could be made. Comparisons of editorial writing with front page news reporting should bring about a better understanding also of the intent of the different paper parts.
4. Let the student select an incident from a fictional story and write a news story about it.
5. Select a current news topic and compare coverage on it from at least three different printed news sources. Comparisons may be suggested in terms of:
   a. Objectivity—facts or opinions;
   b. Words used—neutral or emotion-laden;
   c. Slant—direction if one exists;
   d. Feelings after reading each source.

RESEARCH AND STUDY SKILLS. What better way to teach these skills than to fulfill a need or purpose requiring their application? These skills provide the gifted student with the means to pursue varied and individual interests and to gain a broad background from suggested topics:

1. the history of football, baseball, soccer, tennis or any other sport
2. the background and selected uses of computer technology
3. hydroponics, its limitations and values
4. endangered wildlife, the numbers lost, comparisons of rates of extinction through the years, those species in danger
5. contributions of Charles Steinmetz
6. the life of Shakespeare
7. the Salem witch hunts
8. Howard Carter's discovery of the tomb of King Tut
9. states' rights as an issue of the Civil War
10. Eiffel's great tower
11. a proposed trajectory for a trip to Mars
12. the DNA molecule as a genetic factor.

BOOK DISCUSSIONS. With prior experience in this activity, children at the upper elementary level will be able to broaden and deepen the scope and extent of group book discussions.

1. The relevance of modern social problems as topics may be considered in view of the intended audience, realistic treatment of the topic and individual reactions to specific books.
2. Comparisons of two or more books by the same author may reveal great versatility as well as certain consistencies in style, theme, plot or characterization. Interesting discussions could focus on the likenesses and differences in such books as *Shadow of a Bull* [33] and *A Kingdom in a Horse* [34] by Maia Wojciechowska or the two Newbery Award winners by Elizabeth George Speare, *The Bronze Bow* [35] and *The Witch of Blackbird Pond.* [36]

[33] Maia Wojciechowska, *Shadow of a Bull* (New York, Atheneum, 1965) [c. 1964].

[34] ———, *A Kingdom in a Horse* (New York, Harper & Row, Publishers, 1965).

[35] Elizabeth George Speare, *The Bronze Bow* (Boston, Houghton Mifflin Co., 1961).

[36] ———, *The Witch of Blackbird Pond* (Boston, Houghton Mifflin Co., 1958).

3. The style and effectiveness of plot development in portraying similar themes could be compared. Recognition and meaning of symbols are good areas for discussion, and are highly beneficial to comprehension.

4. The writing style of stories based on primitive settings and characters as *Island of the Blue Dolphins* by Scott O'Dell [37] could be studied and discussed. Analysis of how the author achieved the primitive tone in his writing will aid in the development of a more appreciative and discerning reader. This type of book could be compared with a story placed in a civilized setting and the differences in style forms and words noted and considered by a group.

VOCABULARY ENRICHMENT. Selected topics from the history of the English language will add to the understanding of the language and the ability to use it. An introduction to the use of a thesaurus will be a valuable resource to many gifted students.

1. There are books available for young people that describe the various sources of words and word elements in English such as the book by the Epsteins, *The First Book of Words —Their Family Histories*,[38] *Words from History* [39] and *Words from the Myths*,[40] both by Isaac Asimov. These materials should be supplemented through research at the public library. Charts or transparencies could be made by children for use when discussing the topic in a small group. If a university is near, perhaps an English professor with knowledge in this area would join in a discussion.

2. The contributing factors in the standardization of spelling could be an interesting topic to some students. This study would give youngsters an understanding of existing phoneme-grapheme irregularities. An insight may be gained also into pronunciation clues such as doubled consonants to indicate short vowel sounds (hop—hopped) which may

[37] Scott O'Dell, *Island of the Blue Dolphins* (Boston, Houghton Mifflin Co., 1960).

[38] Sam and Beryl Epstein, *The First Book of Words—Their Family Histories* (New York, Franklin Watts, Inc., 1954).

[39] Isaac Asimov, *Words from History* (Boston, Houghton Mifflin Co., 1968.

[40] ———, *Words from the Myths* (Boston, Houghton Mifflin Co., 1961).

have carried through from a suggested spelling reform in the Middle English period.[41]

3. Through learning about shifts in word meanings, it will become more clear that our language is constantly changing. The changes in meanings of words when used in modern slang would provide a good entry into this topic. The shift in meaning for each word could be classified as one of the four kinds most frequently described:

   a. Specialization, a narrowing of meaning;

   b. Generalization, a broadening of meaning;

   c. Amelioration, an elevation of meaning;

   d. Pejoration, a degeneration of meaning.[42]

   Some youngsters may wish to do additional research on words that have had shifts in meaning. A group compilation of a dictionary citing the meaning changes of words may be a highly interesting project.

4. During a brief introduction of a thesaurus and its use, the teacher may call attention to subtle shifts of meaning in a sentence or phrase caused by the selection of a particular synonym for a word. The word "reject," for example, may be given greater specificity according to the situation by substituting it with exclude, eject, repudiate or refuse. A thesaurus should be kept in the classroom so gifted youngsters may have use of it. Encouragement should be given to these youngsters to use the thesaurus to increase the preciseness of written reports or creative writing.

Summary

Enrichment in reading for the gifted does not mean adding projects or "extras" to the regular curriculum; it must be the regular curriculum for these youngsters.

In this chapter, an attempt has been made to suggest types of activities and experiences which would add depth to comprehension, breadth to vocabulary and stimulate the child toward critical and creative thinking. For general guidance, ideas were

[41] L. M. Myers, *The Roots of Modern English* (Boston, Little, Brown and Co., 1966), pp. 135–137.

[42] *Ibid.*, pp. 245–249.

arranged into level placement sections designated as early primary, middle elementary and upper elementary with many variations of levels expected.

Several ideas were presented to increase the comprehension of young children through introducing and studying plot structure and development, theme identification, characterization styles and poetry form and meter.

Story motifs, cultural effects on literature, literary forms, more complex plot structures, theme and characterization comparisons, identification of story elements, the study of animals as characters, the consideration of style factors and the use of research and study skills were the bases of ideas presented for the middle elementary level.

Ideas for the continued development of the understanding of factors concerned with plot, theme, setting, style and characterization were suggested. Interpreting cultural factors through stories, continued study of literary forms with appropriate depth, an emphasis on critical reading and research and study skills and topics from the history of the English language for vocabulary enrichment, plus creative endeavors summarize the direction of experiences for academically gifted upper elementary students.

CHAPTER VI

READING IN THE CONTENT AREAS

EVERY CHILD, gifted or not is required to do extensive reading in many content areas. To accomplish this goal he must develop satisfactory word analysis and comprehension skills. He should gain the understanding, for example, that the problems and challenges confronted in reading science material are quite different from reading fictional articles.

In order to help the gifted child succeed in reading content materials, the following topics are discussed in this chapter: reading competencies needed for reading content materials; content reading in the primary and intermediate grades and reading content materials in the junior and senior high school.

Reading Competencies Needed for Reading Content Materials

Through observation and the use of formal and informal devices, teachers can determine if gifted pupils possess the necessary skills for extensive content reading. A teacher can be of much help to a learner if she understands the nature of the skills needed and where his strengths and limitations may be with respect to these skills. The competencies noted in the following section were determined after examining the data obtained from careful observations of gifted pupils, interviews with teachers and reading specialists and from numerous professional articles on the subject.

A. *The reader must be able to assimilate numerous facts and figures in such areas as mathematics, science, and social studies.* The ability to develop a broad mind-set which will allow a reader to cope with complex concepts proves to be bewildering for many. Many have dealt mainly with fictional material using a rapid reading rate. Teachers can aid pupils to comprehend these materials by giving them purposes for reading and supplying them with reading matter which is challenging and suited to their needs and interests. It is especially important for the gifted child to have specific questions or purposes in mind before undertaking a reading assignment in content areas. The teacher can help him to understand that content books often vary considerably with respect to difficulty both within a single book and among several volumes. The student should have a clear understanding of additional resources which may be available for clarification of difficult concepts which may be encountered in regular content books.

B. *Pupils must demonstrate that they can differentiate between fact and opinion and identify various propaganda techniques.* The gifted child is usually efficient in the mastery of critical reading skills; however, he is not immune to believing what he reads in a given book or journal is the absolute truth. He needs to understand that such items as editorials and journal articles are the opinions of the writer and are not necessarily factual in nature. He needs to train himself to ask several questions:

1. What is the copyright date of the book or article? Assuming that some of the information might have been assembled as much as a year previous to the publication date, what effect does this aspect have on the believability of the writer's expressions?

2. Does the writer employ one or more propaganda techniques to convey a given position? The teacher should help the gifted reader to identify such techniques as the "plain folks device," "name calling," "the transfer device," "card stacking," "bandwagon approach" and "identification with prestige." (The child should understand that these techniques may or may not be desirable, depending upon the intent of the person or persons employing the devices.)

3. What are the qualifications of the writer and what appears to be his purpose for compiling the material? Pupils should be alterted to the fact that many persons produce selections

for popular consumption and have little, if any, background of experience or training for such an assignment. They should be alterted to read the author's background information often found on the dust covers of books. Additional information can often be found in special resource books such as *Who's Who In America.*

4. Does the writer include supportive data for his conclusions which he proposes? Pupils should be alerted to look for such sweeping generalizations as "the crime rate among middle class white people in cities under 3,000 population is much lower than is true with white people in cities over 3,000 population." To make such a statement obviously calls for substantial proof such as data secured from well-controlled studies. Content area materials, especially in the area of social studies, often contain materials of this type. Information found in one book should be compared with data found in other volumes.

5. Is the material written for a particular class of people? Some materials are designed, for example, to be humorous and satirical in nature, and are not intended to be factual or literal in nature. The reader needs to understand these possibilities and be alert to them.

C. *The reader must be able to pronounce and understand the meaning of sizable numbers of new and difficult words introduced in a brief amount of space.* Gifted readers should be challenged to read a variety of books and magazines and to increase their overall vocabulary level. Science and mathematics materials may contain such difficult words as "coefficient," "translucent" and "convection." Many textbook authors assume the reader can understand these words and place them in their proper context. Teachers should emphasize that the glossary, dictionary and other aids should be consulted if proper understanding of such words is to be realized. (There is information in another part of this chapter regarding activities for vocabulary enlargement.)

D. *The ability to understand and correlate a large number of unrelated facts and principles is an important skill to be developed by gifted children.* In a history text, for example, the child may find a discussion regarding the tariff policies of six different U. S. Presidents. The span of time relating to this concept may cover as much as forty years; however, all of the data may be developed in as few as four or five pages. Such material, if it is to be understood, must be placed into some type of meaningful mind-set which will allow the learner to remember a sequence of events. The use of outlines and carefully prepared notes will help to accomplish this objective. The pupil should have definite purposes in mind when reading content material so he can determine what information should be remembered and what data can be ignored. These purposes should originate with the reader (depending on his own personal need), the teacher and an occasional question which may be suggested by the author of a source book.

E. *The gifted reader should develop a flexible reading rate which will allow him to skim quickly for a single idea or read slowly to remember many significant details.* Many persons, including otherwise able readers, labor under the assumption that there is *one* best reading speed. If they have been influenced by speed reading advocates, they may feel compelled to skim all reading matter at hundreds or thousands of words per minute. Pupils must remember that reading rate *must be flexible* and determined by the *purposes* of the reader.

For example, if he wishes to find only the information relating to the ingredients found in a chemical mixture, he should have the ability to scan the table in the appendices of the volume where this information is found. This particular procedure may entail as many as 2,000 words and consume less than a minute. On the other hand, if reading for details is desired, as few as 75 to 100 words may be read per minute. There is no one best speed to use for all kinds of reading, since the reader must keep in mind that he has the obligation to maintain a two-way track of communication with the writer. For example, if a given author wishes to explain a very detailed process and uses a sizable number of difficult concepts, the student cannot communicate effectively if he insists on trying to "read" at a speed involving hundreds or thousands of words.

F. *The reader must have a working knowledge of where to find and how to use various source books and media devices which will help him to fully understand content area materials.* The gifted child should be encouraged to read widely in special source books for additional information regarding specific topics. The construction of research papers should employ the utilization of such materials and devices as special encyclopedias, the *World Almanac,* the *Reader's Guide to Periodical Literature,* the card catalogue and atlases of various kinds. Specific lessons must be provided by classroom teachers to insure that a body of knowledge has been accumulated regarding these sources. Unfortunately, educators are sometimes guilty of keeping pupils so busy they have little time for using specialized materials.

Content Reading in the Primary and Intermediate Grades

In the primary and intermediate grade levels, the majority of the reading tasks demanded of pupils consists of reading fictional and human interest selections from basal readers and weekly children's papers. Fortunately, most manuals or teacher editions which accompany these materials contain numerous helps for the enlargement of vocabulary skills and general comprehension. Words which are probably new or different for the children are listed for "special" attention. Guiding questions are frequently suggested which will aid the learner in reading for a purpose and gaining word and sentence meaning. The young child who is especially precocious has a natural desire to explore many sources for additional information about various topics which intrigue him. These pupils deserve maximum help from teachers in their search for new knowledge.

There are a few pieces of reading matter in the content areas which the young gifted child reads requiring guidance and help from the classroom teacher. The suggestions in the next major section have been classroom tested by innovative teachers. While it is assumed that not *all* of the activities will be equally useful to all readers of this volume, many can be employed with definite success.

A. *A large variety of materials which represent a number of reading levels and various subjects must be made available.* In some cases, a workable arrangement may be constructed whereby primary teachers may borrow books and resource volumes from the middle grade teachers for use by gifted readers. The reverse procedure may be used in order that retarded readers in the middle grades may have access to easier reading matter from primary rooms.

Suggestions with respect to the kinds of books, magazines and resource volumes which might be purchased are included in the appendices section of this book. The authors wish to emphasize that no personal endorsement is intended or implied regarding any one material; however, these aids are being used by professionals in different locations with success. The selection of materials obviously will depend on such matters as budget limitations and the number of pupils who can and should make use of these sources. Before large purchases of any one type of material are made, a pilot study should be conducted to test its efficiency with local pupils. The frank recommendations of local and area teachers who have used given materials should be solicited.

B. *Readability formulas should be employed to determine the difficulty of materials.* Many companies supply information relating to this data; however, some firms do not. The *Dale-Chall, Flesch,* or *Fry* formulas may be used. (Information concerning these formulas can be obtained from volumes by Bond and Tinker,[1] Harris[2] and Dechant.[3]) The gifted child should be given many choices of reading matter at and above his instructional reading level. (Instructional reading is defined in this volume as that level where a given child can read orally with 95 to 97 per cent accuracy and demonstrate at *least* 75 per cent proficiency in silent reading comprehension.)

In light of the previous remarks, a primary or intermediate teacher of gifted children should have source materials available with reading difficulty levels up to the high school or even

[1] Guy L. Bond and Miles A. Tinker, *Reading Difficulties: Their Diagnosis and Correction.* 3rd Ed. (New York, Appleton-Century-Crofts, 1973).

[2] Albert J. Harris, *How to Increase Reading Ability* (New York, McKay, 1970).

[3] Emerald V. Dechant, *Diagnosis and Remediation of Reading Disability* (West Nyack, Parker, 1968).

college levels. Occasionally, there are high achieving pupils in the third grade who can understand the content of upper grade and high school encyclopedias such as the *Encyclopedia Americana* or *Encyclopaedia Brittannica*. (The names of the publishers of these aids can be found in the appendix section.)

C. *One of the most important goals of the reading program in the content areas is that of building a substantial and useful vocabulary.* Young children, and most especially gifted children, normally possess an intense desire to learn new words. They want to impress their peers and parents with this newfound knowledge and thus build their egos and self-image.

The following creative procedures may be employed by teachers for building vocabulary skills of precocious children:

1. Place the new words on the chalkboard and help the pupils understand the correct pronunciation for each word or phrase. Illustrate the meaning of the words and phrases by providing study sheets which contain sentences in which the meanings are clearly indicated. Note, for example, that meanings change from chapter to chapter as in the case of the word, "mandate." Call attention to the fact that the election of a given government official may have been referred to as a "mandate of the people" in a previous chapter, but the word "mandate" in the phrase, "a German mandate" in the present chapter has an entirely different meaning. Unless pupils are alerted to these transitional meanings, they may well form a single meaning and be quite confused when the word is presented in a different context.

2. Another procedure for improving vocabulary is to have children study Latin derivatives, prefixes and suffixes. Illustrate, for example, the meanings of such prefixes as "mono" and "tri," as in the words "monoplane" and "triangle," in order to establish that "mono" means one and that "tri" means three.

3. Encourage pupils to construct and use a personal file of new vocabulary words which have been encountered. Using his own dictionary, the student should indicate the correct pronunciation of each word, the several meanings which the word might have (particularly within the scope of the social studies topics) and how it might be used in a sentence.

4. Serious dictionary study may be developed around a study topic in social studies. During the study, pupils should be asked to select the one meaning which applies to a particular word found in a contextual situation. Many authors of social studies material provide glossaries which should be used as a major tool in diction-

ary word study—in fact, glossaries may well be used as a primary source and the dictionary as a secondary source.[4]

D. *Since the end product of all reading instruction is gaining meaning from the printed page, careful direction should be given to able children in order for them to develop maximum ability in the total area of comprehension.* Pupils should understand that they should have a well-defined purpose or question in mind before they undertake a reading assignment in one or more source books, magazines, or papers. Teachers should guide pupils to ask themselves the following questions: "What specific information am I looking for?" "Am I likely to find this data in this material as indicated by the table of contents and index?" "Do I need to read slowly for details or can I skim and scan the materials until the exact piece of information is found?"

Several of the activities in the next section have been used effectively by creative teachers for enlarging comprehension skills of gifted elementary children. The teacher should adapt or adopt those ideas which appear to be most practical for his situation.

1. Call attention to the glossary and other specialized sections of a resource volume and demonstrate how to use these tools to gain further meaning with regard to a given topic. Check to see that they understand how to use the maps, graphs and charts. They may be encouraged to enlarge these devices for use by the total class. A student's talents may be utilized to make similar illustrations for the school or classroom newspaper using data obtained from the coach regarding records from a school track meet or from the principal regarding attendance or enrollment information of the school.

2. Develop (with the aid of pupils) a series of crossword puzzles which involve concepts being considered in a lesson or unit. Pupils can exchange these in a given room or a school-wide program can be instituted which would involve many students.

[4] From the book, *Reading Improvement in The Elementary School* by Donald C. Cushenbery. © 1969 by Parker Publishing Co., Inc., West Nyack, New York and used with their permission.

3. To give able students a firm knowledge of how to adjust speed of reading to reading purpose, an exercise such as the following may be utilized:

   Directions: Sometimes we need to read very slowly to find certain information. Other times it is possible to read at an "average" speed. Often we can read quickly or scan if we want to find a single fact. On the blank to the left of each statement, write one of the words, *slow, average,* or *fast* which tells best how you should read for the assignment which is described.

   _____ a. Find the name of the U. S. President who served from 1920–1924.

   _____ b. Give the names of the four cars which are described on pages 21 and 22.

   _____ c. What war is mentioned in the title of the fiction book?

   _____ d. List the names of the fifteen ingredients which are described on page 62.

   _____ e. What are the names of the three baseball stars which are mentioned in the third chapter?

4. Encourage creative pupils to construct time lines or sequence charts after reading a history or science selection. They can share these projects with other pupils and all will have a better understanding of the total concepts the teacher hopes will be learned.

5. Emphasize the importance of finding answers to "who," "what," "when," "why," and "where" when reading newspaper articles. A pupil who is artistically talented may wish to construct a bulletin board display showing a newspaper with lines running from the "5W" captions to the appropriate lines which correlate with the correct "W."

6. The authors of this volume have concluded that too many gifted readers are not making appropriate use of outlining procedures. Young children in the primary grades can be taught to use a simple outlining procedure which will enable them to double and sometimes triple their level of comprehension.

Reading Content Materials in the Junior
and Senior High School

The reading competencies listed earlier in this chapter are as applicable for junior and senior high students as they are for elementary pupils. A few of the suggestions listed in the previous section can also be adapted for use with older and more able pupils. In addition to these suggestions, the ideas in the following section have been used by successful teachers of gifted junior and senior high students.

A. Particular guidance should be given to students with respect to the location and use of specialized materials available to them. Creative students are not usually satisfied with a single book as a source of information. Teachers should inform these students by word of mouth and through the use of handouts about the location of supplementary aids. In most cases the local city or university library contains a rich storehouse of information relating to a topic or subject which might be under study by a given learner. Content area teachers have a responsibility to acquaint all students (especially *able* readers) about these sources.

B. In some schools the use of a "contract" system has been employed to encourage gifted readers to read widely in the content areas. Under this type of program an "honors" or "A" grade is promised if a certain assignment is completed which entails the use of X number of references. Not all students are motivated by this type of activity, but many are challenged by the approach.

C. The use of a five-step reading approach such as the following helps insure that the reader will achieve maximum meaning from a given body of printed matter. The lesson plan which follows explains the numerous possibilities in employing a method of this type.

Title of Unit: THE WESTWARD MOVEMENT

Step I: Readiness and/or Survey Stage

At the beginning of the first lesson the teacher should generate interest in the topic by asking such questions as "What do you suppose is meant by 'The Westward Movement'?" "What groups of people were involved and why did they want to move west?" The map of the United States as it was constituted in the mid-nineteenth century might be displayed to show which states had been established and what areas were left to be developed as future states. A further discussion might take place regarding the character and nature of the pioneers who settled the western part of our country.

The use of a 16 mm. film such as "West to California" might serve as an interest arouser. Another idea might be the engagement of a museum director . . . who would show early artifacts and explain their importance.

New words or phrases should be introduced at this point:

A. The *Conestoga* wagon was a major means of transporting goods.

B. Many *renegrades* from the United States Army *infiltrated* the ranks of the pioneers.

C. The *bushwhacker* was a constant enemy of the trailriders. (Note that the words and phrases are enclosed *in* sentences for maximum meaning.)

Step II: Reading Purpose Stage

If the teacher is to help students derive various kinds of meaning from selections, guiding questions must be constructed which will serve as purposes for reading. Some questions should come from the students after they have had a chance to scan chapter headings and sub-topics of the resource book which are available for the unit. The teacher may have very specific questions he would like the class to use. Other questions may be borrowed from the close of a resource text chapter.

For the unit under consideration, the following questions may be representative:

A. What motives did the pioneers have for moving to the westward areas?

B. How was the Kansas-Nebraska territory settled and divided into states?

C. What were the provisions of the Medicine Lodge (Kansas)

Indian Peace Treaty which was signed between the five Plains Indian tribes and the U. S. Government?

D. What is meant by "staking a claim?"

Step III: Silent Reading Stage

For the silent reading which takes place both in and out of the regular classroom, the class text and various other sources should be used by the students in accordance with their *current* reading levels. The teacher should not be concerned about which book the students use to find the answers to the guiding questions. Information should be given to the students regarding which books are available and how these books will help them. (It is assumed that the librarian has helped the teacher select books from the library stacks appropriate for the unit.)

Step IV: The Discussion Stage

During the discussion stage, the responses to the questions which were devised at Step III are given. Oral and silent re-reading for any one of several purposes may be appropriate. When no student has been able to find a satisfactory answer to a question, the teacher may wish to have groups of students engage in silent re-reading of certain pages in the text or other sources where the answer is certain to be found. In other cases, silent re-reading may be necessary in order to substantiate an answer given by a student which appears to be in disagreement with data discovered by the teacher or other students.

Oral re-reading might be useful in reconstructing the exact meaning of a sentence or paragraph. Voice inflections and pitch can add much meaning to various types of reading materials.

Step V: Reviewing and Application Stage

As a final procedure, the teacher should employ various instructional methods to insure that the students understand the relationship of the material presented in this lesson with the information which has been discussed in previous units.

One successful instructor asked a committee of students to construct a continuing time line which would help them remember the names of the Presidents, tenure, acts passed during their stay in office, etc.

The use of resource speakers and films to achieve application of meaning may be pertinent. The production of a video-tape with students role-playing important historical figures is an ingenious, innovative procedure. The production could be used as a part of the school's American Education Week activities.[5]

Summary

A number of competencies are needed if a gifted reader is to gain maximum understanding from reading content area materials. Pupils at all grade levels should be encouraged to read widely and enlarge their vocabulary and comprehension skill levels. The suggestions noted in this chapter can be of much help to the teacher in planning for the reading instructional needs of able pupils.

[5] From the book, *Remedial Reading in The Secondary School* by Donald C. Cushenbery. © 1972 by Parker Publishing Co., Inc., West Nyack, New York and used with their permission.

CHAPTER VII

READING PROGRAMS FOR THE GIFTED AT THE SECONDARY LEVEL

I N MOST SCHOOLS there is a lack of an identifiable reading program for gifted secondary students. In too many instances, the more able learner is taught in the same manner as the average student. The purpose of this chapter is to outline some of the goals and characteristics of a desirable program and to describe some of the projects which have been undertaken in various school systems in the United States. While it is expected that no one program or project can be transported in its entirety to another location, various facets can be employed in a number of situations with a high level of success.

Characteristics and Goals of the Programs

Regardless of the program undertaken, various goals should be established if the reading needs of gifted students are met.

A. *At the outset, a careful analysis of the reading skill development levels of each student must be undertaken.* Reading programs, whether for the gifted or retarded, must be individualized in order to plan an instructional program which will have maximum value to each learner. After a student has been identified as an able student, appropriate standardized and informal evaluation devices should be implemented. The next chapter of this volume contains suggestions with respect to the names of tests which might be employed. The final decision should rest on such factors as number of students and their age range.

An analysis sheet for each learner should be compiled to show such aspects as instructional reading level, independent reading level, vocabulary proficiency, comprehension development and rate of reading. This information must be made available for all teachers and other professionals who have contact with the identified able student.

B. *Every secondary teacher of students should understand that it is his responsibility to plan and execute lessons which will challenge the gifted to work at maximum levels in terms of their reading skill capacities.* To insure that this goal is achieved, each instructor needs to secure a wide variety of learning and reading aids which are motivating in nature. This practice would demand the placement of university level books and magazines in the secondary library and classrooms. The students should be informed of these sources by their teachers. Special instruction regarding how to use the sources may be useful and practical.

C. *Teachers involved in challenging gifted students to improve reading skills should understand that not all persons learn the same way and that these pupils need to be exposed to many different learning modalities.* Many types of approaches should be used including the aural, visual and kinesthetic methods. The vast media sources available from major companies allow the educator to have an opportunity to construct a unique and individual learning program package. Discovering which modality is most useful with a given student necessitates the use of formal and informal testing devices and careful observation on the part of teachers.

D. *Meeting the special reading instructional needs of secondary students must be a common goal shared by all teachers who instruct able learners.* In too many instances the impression is given by teachers that the job of reading instruction at the high school level is the responsibility of the English department. Every teacher who makes use of any printed matter in class must understand that reading skill development is everyone's job. If the able student is to be motivated and challenged to his maximum level of learning, then every teacher must be a part of the instructional team.

E. *Rigid, uniform reading assignments should not be applied to the instructional program for the gifted.* In English classes, is it really necessary to insist that *all* students read all of the books on the "must" list? The author takes the point of view that every student should have some acquaintance with the world's treasury of great literature; however, the imposition of long lists of required reading for the creative, able learner is highly debatable. The love of literature and the joy of reading widely for fun and relaxation have been effectively terminated in many instances by teachers who take an unyielding, unreasonable viewpoint with respect to classwide assignments of this type. Long written book reports should not be required unless the student has a genuine interest in wanting to share the contents of the volume with his peers. There are many suitable alternatives to the traditional written book report which should be employed.

F. *Educators should be careful to keep each student informed of his individual strengths and limitations with regard to the total body of reading skills.* The student should understand the implications from test data compiled for him and how this information was used to build his particular instructional program. This responsibility could be shared jointly by teachers, counselors and any other persons who are a part of the school staff.

G. *The reading program developed for the able pupil should be described in the form of a printed document so all interested persons (teachers, parents, students) will have a clear understanding of the instructional goals which are undertaken.* Many programs for the gifted (and for other types of pupils) never really achieve desired levels of competency because they are not fully understood by the persons who are most directly responsible for their success. Conversely, some outstanding programs are not transported to other school districts because the information has not been refined and published and thus cannot be mailed to interested parties.

H. *Adequate and definite provisions should be made to allow each student to evaluate the reading instructional program that has been employed with him.* The age of accountability demands that the able, creative and imaginative student be given a chance to critique his program. Serious and conscientious educators can make effective and practical use of this information to construct the best possible future set of reading experiences available.

Types of Reading Programs for Gifted
Secondary Students

At the time of publication, a significant number of secondary schools were engaged in planning and executing reading programs for gifted and creative students. These programs have been designed to meet the particular needs of the pupils involved and involve several different kinds of curricular approaches. Briefly summarized, these programs can be put in twelve categories:

A. *Classroom Enrichment.* Each teacher in each of the content areas diversifies his or her instruction to allow gifted students to pursue creative projects using materials beyond the textbook. Of all of the approaches described in this section, this one is probably one of the most valuable.

B. *Acceleration.* Under this plan, the high school student is allowed to move ahead to an advanced course in a discipline if he can demonstrate that he has gained the competencies normally required of those who work at the elementary level. The latter aspect can be adjudged by formal and informal tests and by observation.

C. *Special Sections Grouping.* Under this arrangement, students are grouped heterogeneously during any given half-day for various classes, while during the other half-day they are grouped in special instructional divisions or classes for those who are classified as gifted. Usually these classes have been designed for small enrollments and much interaction among students is encouraged and expected.

D. *Additional Credit Courses.* Some school administrators allow able students to enroll in extra courses to give them added experiences for future academic training in a college or university center. The titles of these courses are varied in order to meet the needs and tastes of students. Offerings include such subjects as "Ecology in the Mid-Plains," "Classical Music," "American Political Parties" and "Rapid Reading Skills." School officials often require that a student maintain at least a grade of "B" or better in his required courses in order to participate in the additional credit courses. Generally speaking a minimum number of students must enroll in a course for it to be offered. A course may be offered on request if there is a sufficient number of students who enroll in the course and if a teacher can be found to instruct.

E. *Program of Early Admission.* A gifted student may be allowed to enroll in high school or college courses at an earlier age than usual if he can demonstrate by test data that he is capable of competing with older students. There was a fear among some educators that younger students would be at a social disadvantage with older students when the early admission policy was instituted. There appears to be adequate research evidence to refute such fears, since the major interest of the students involved appears to be academic challenge.

F. *Telescoped Curriculum Design.* Some school districts allow particularly able students to complete courses in a shorter period of time. Summer school courses as well as evening classes provide an opportunity to complete a three-year high school program in a two-year period. Exceptionally gifted students can sometimes reduce the time limit under two years.

G. *Interclassroom Grouping.* This plan allows each teacher to group students on the basis of ability in order to diversify instructional techniques and materials. Theoretically, each group of learners can move at its own rate and the learners are not held back or pushed to perform tasks which they cannot achieve. Students feel comfortable with this arrangement because success is realized quickly.

H. *Credit by Examination.* Some high schools and many universities allow able students to take comprehensive standardized and informal tests in certain subject areas to determine academic competency in the areas in question. If a high score is achieved on the evaluative measures, the student is allowed credit for the course and formal enrollment is waived. It is possible in some instances to earn as many as four high school credits and thirty college semester hours' credit by this means.

I. *Non-Academic Interest Groups.* Students with the same or nearly the same interests and academic levels are urged to join other students with similar characteristics. These groups explore interests relating to foreign language, drama, literature, art, crafts, music, history and religion. Meeting rooms are provided in the school building and meetings are conducted at times (including evenings and Saturdays) which are most convenient to the students. Usually school administrators require that at least one faculty member must serve as an advisor to the group.

J. *Special Course Offerings.* When test data and other information point to the fact that a sizable number of gifted students are in evidence in a given building, there may be provisions made for offering special courses which have a common appeal to these students. Courses such as the following may be offered for this purpose: "Marriage and the Family," "Money and Budgets," "Rock Music in the Modern Age," "American Political Parties," "Advanced Physiology" and "Race Car Construction." Practical considerations such as the availability of qualified faculty members and classroom space dictate the extent to which these courses can be offered.

K. *Non-Credit Seminars.* In some cases special seminars or workshops are conducted for especially able students. The time spent in these activities is usually two to four weeks in duration or until student objectives have been met. Very often these activities are conducted by community leaders not professionally trained as teachers. They may be bankers, doctors, store managers, farmers or sports figures. In many instances these people donate their time for this service. The activities may or may not take place on the school campus and may be scheduled at times other than usual school hours. Costs connected with such offerings are often borne by local civic groups as a part of their community service program.

L. *Honors Courses.* Courses of this type are usually required with materials and techniques geared to the able student. Advanced level materials are used along with more technical media devices. More topics and subjects are studied than in general or average courses.

Regardless of the plan used to accommodate the secondary gifted reader, a number of admonitions must be kept in mind if maximum motivation is to be obtained. These students tend to learn better through association and abstract reading and not by rote learning processes. Relationships between concepts and ideas are generally easy to perceive. Gifted students tend to be curious, imaginative, original and creative in most undertakings.

These students like to work individually; however, they are not adverse to preparing and giving oral reports and sharing exciting experiences which they have encountered. In literature, they have a natural inclination to write creative poetry and prose which may have abstract qualities. In most school experiences they exhibit a much more advanced level of maturity than is true of the average student.

For each student to realize his fullest potential requires much study and thought on the part of the educator. The items discussed previously and the aspects noted in the following section must be kept in mind at all times.

1. Materials used in any program must always be at a sufficiently challenging level.

2. Certain reading skill components such as critical reading, interpretative reading, use of technical aids and literary appreciation should be introduced at a much earlier time in the language arts curriculum than is the case with most average readers. Students can and should develop the ability to detect the writer's purpose and intent, his style and inferences designed to play on the emotions of the reader.

3. In the development of any reading program for the gifted special attention should be given to the sensing of relationships, drawing conclusions and inferences and relating various abstract concepts together into a meaningful mindset. Memorizing and reciting unrelated details should be given a minor role. The special student must always be given the opportunity to criticize and evaluate his primary and secondary reading sources.

4. All units of study which require a large amount of reading and research must always be problem-centered. The student should feel he has the freedom to explore and use large numbers of reading materials found in the school or home library. The teacher has an ever-continuing responsibility for recommending types of books to meet his needs.
5. The program selected must motivate the student to desire intrinsic rewards as opposed to extrinsic materialistic rewards. The feeling of self-satisfaction is one of the most significant positive reinforcers.
6. Reading and related language arts activities must be undertaken in a relaxed atmosphere devoid of rigid and tight schedules, traditional evaluation and lecture-oriented teaching. The curriculum for the very able student must be as individualized as possible.
7. A natural outgrowth of any reading program should be the intense desire to engage in leisure time reading. Large numbers of books in all of the content areas must be available at all times.
8. There must be an adequate opportunity for the student to have a forum for displaying the knowledge he has gained from reading widely. Suggestions might be the use of panel discussions, plays, tape recordings, video-tape recordings and radio and television programs. Arts and crafts projects which are necessary outgrowths of a given unit may be a useful technique to employ.
9. Any reading curriculum for the gifted must contain adequate blocks of free time for independent research and leisure time reading. Books and other sources for these activities should not be required by the teacher.
10. The gifted student should be allowed the time and opportunity to discuss his viewpoints and support them with appropriate data.

Descriptions of Programs for Gifted Secondary Students

Of all the programs described earlier in this chapter, the use of the seminar approach appears to be the one most commonly used. One such program described by Jackman and Bachtold [1] took place in the junior high school at Davis, California.

A very careful appraisal of student needs was undertaken. It was discovered that even though the gifted students were enrolled in advanced courses and had other enriching experiences, a number felt they needed further challenge. With this in mind the staff decided to establish a series of seminar meetings with operational guidelines adapted from the counseling-instructional program in the California Project Talent. Grades, credits and homework were not required and only those students who scored in the upper two percent of a group intelligence test and a reading or mathematics test could be considered by the program director. The program was designed purposely with a limited amount of structure to allow as much flexibility as possible. Though the seminars had a number of goals, the development of communication skills was one of the major objectives.

Out of approximately 500 students enrolled in the school, a total of eighty-two students were eligible and accepted the invitation to become a member of the seminar groups. The seminars were scheduled bi-monthly on a staggered period schedule in order that any one student would not miss the same content lesson during the period. Two large seminar groups were established.

Many of the seminar presentations were devoted to topics chosen by the pupils themselves. Most topics extended beyond one class meeting.

At the end of the seminar sessions, students were invited to give their reactions with regard to the value of the sessions as they affected their educational growth. Of those responding, 93 percent said the seminars had been worthwhile and 91 percent indicated a desire to participate in the activities during the next school year.

The Portland, Oregon school system has had identifiable programs for exceptionally endowed high school students for several

---

[1] William D. Jackman and Louise M. Bachtold, "Evaluation of a Seminar for Gifted Junior High Students," *The Gifted Child Quarterly*, XIII (Autumn, 1969), pp. 163–167.

years. According to Southworth, Leavens and Schukart [2] there are
a number of curricular provisions made for these students in the
area of English and literature. They have double-period classes
which combine English and social studies, seminars and regularly sized high ability classes which use more difficult materials.
There is a common emphasis in all of these classes which stresses
inter-student discussions with the teacher acting as a critical par-
ticipant instead of presiding as a judge.

Numerous types of activities were used in English–Social
Studies. One year a unit on "The Idea of a General Education"
was used. Various selections by Arnold, Bacon, Carlyle, Dewey,
Hill and Newman were read and discussed. This was followed by
an eleven-week study of Greek history, literature and philosophy.
During this period they read materials by Homer, Thucydides
and Plato. A unit was also developed regarding the Renaissance
and involved readings by Machiavelli and Montaigne.

Any seminar or class developed for the gifted secondary student should be flexible and contain much variety. In the area of
reading, the following is a suggested list of activities which may
be incorporated:

    A. Evaluate library source materials with regard to their uses
       in undertaking different kinds of research projects. The
       students could investigate such matters as copyright dates
       and the background of the writers or compilers.

    B. Investigate biographical printed materials to develop an
       appreciation for the services and contributions of leading
       persons in today's society.

    C. Read a broad range of books and magazines to gain in-
       sights with respect to new hobbies or activities which might
       be undertaken.

    D. Learn to identify various literary styles exhibited in poetry,
       novels, biographies, essays and short stories.

    E. Explore large numbers of books and magazines which con-
       tain articles dealing with current social and political issues.

[2] Mabel D. Southworth, L. Dolores Leavens and Janice Schukart, *English and Literature Classes for Exceptionally Endowed Students in the High Schools of Portland, Oregon.* (Unpublished document), February, 1957.

F. Read numerous selections of prose and poetry from different time periods and analyze and compare them with regard to style and content.

G. Determine the author's goals and/or values and compare them with the reader's when a particular topic is explored.

H. Build ever-increasing sight, listening, speaking, and writing vocabularies.

Related language arts activities in the areas of writing and listening may be a part of a gifted student's seminar or class. Some of these activities are included in the next section. The number of activities which may be included in any offering will necessarily be governed by the number of students involved, their interests and the amount and kind of resources available.

A. *Listening Activities*

1. Listen to scheduled debates and newscasts and discuss the facts and opinions given.

2. Evaluate the speaking performances of literary and political figures to discover errors in speech, redundancy and range of vocabulary.

3. Conduct a study of everyday noises about school and homes to gain some insight relative to the possible effect of noise pollution on students in particular and the public in general.

4. Listen and try to determine how various sound effects are made in a movie or other production shown on television or seen on stage.

B. *Writing Activities*

1. Prepare bibliographies of leading local civic and political figures. These may be used by the school or city newspaper.

2. Create dramatizations and original plays which may be used in a talent show sponsored by the local school activities council.

3. Display through writing the meaning and importance of various forms and techniques used in journalism such as editorials, feature articles, syndicated columns and advertisements.

4. Organize and summarize advanced reading materials

so that the average reader may enjoy and appreciate the same types of reading materials as the able student.

Summary

A number of characteristics and goals should be established for any type of reading program formulated for the gifted. These include evaluation of skill development, promotion of challenging and varied lessons, enlargement of reading skills by all faculty members and evaluation of pupil progress by the learner himself.

There are many types of programs available to meet the needs of the gifted reader. Special sections grouping, credit courses, non-credit courses, seminars, interclassroom grouping and telescoped curriculum design constitute a partial list of possibilities.

Programs for the gifted may take any one of several forms. Some of these possibilities are discussed in the latter part of this chapter.

CHAPTER VIII

EVALUATING READING
PROGRESS

THE PROCESS OF EVALUATION is an important component of the reading program, since these processes provide the teacher with data relating to the effectiveness of the reading program in accomplishing desired results. The principles involved in such procedures as they relate to the gifted child are very similar to those which might be applied to the so-called "average" student.

In planning a program of reading instruction for these children, a very careful diagnosis of each learner's present reading strengths and limitations must be undertaken through the use of commercial and informal tests. This procedure will allow educators to construct a learning program which will fit the exact needs of the student in question. If he has potential for greater growth in reading than displayed by test data, then additional appropriate action must be taken.

After a survey test has been given and the scores have been analyzed, a practical reading program based on the particular needs of a child must be constructed. With the gifted child, this should involve the use of diagnostic-prescriptive teaching methods on an individual basis as much as staff and resources permit. The curriculum constructed for any given student should be considered flexible.

At a given point after an instructional program has been in use for several weeks or months, a new set of evaluation procedures should be instituted to measure the effectiveness of the instructional program. If basic limitations are discovered, the teaching procedures can be changed or recycled to better meet the needs of the students in question.

This chapter is concerned with a number of topics. In the first part of the chapter, the purposes of evaluation are discussed; in the second part, standardized and informal tests are described; and in the third part, a number of suggestions are given relative to the administration of commercial tests.

Purposes of Evaluation

The total reading curriculum for any child should be based on a thorough evaluation of his present strengths and limitations in order to design a program which will challenge him to reach his potential in all of the major reading skill areas. The structuring of an extensive evaluation sequence is not an easy job since it entails many competencies on the part of the teacher. Among other things, he needs to have a broad knowledge of the types of tests available, the purposes of the instruments, the scoring procedures involved and proper interpretation of the data derived. Evaluation is one of the most important phases of the reading instructional program and it is the hope of the authors that the material contained in this chapter will help the teacher of the gifted to assume his proper role in this aspect of instruction.

Purposes of Evaluation

1. *Evaluation techniques should be employed to aid the teacher in determining the exact instructional needs of his pupils.* The information derived from a group survey or individual diagnostic test might be the major criteria used in determining whether the reading instructional program should stress phonics, reading for details or any of the major reading components. The test data from a survey test will serve to identify those students who possess superior reading skills. If computerized scoring is used, the machines will provide a "read-out," for example, of the names of the students whose reading skill levels are two or three grade levels above enrolled grade level. This information aids the teacher immensely in identifying those students who may be gifted in reading. Further instruments can be administered to substantiate or refute the initial findings from the survey test. All of the data should be of help to the teacher in constructing

activities which will tend to be enriching and motivating to the more able student.

2. *Evaluation instruments can provide invaluable information to the teacher with respect to appropriate grouping of students for instructional purposes.* There is some evidence to suggest that more able students who are grouped homogeneously may reach higher levels of achievement because they are challenged by peers with similar abilities. In this kind of learning environment, the teacher may be able to use a common core of teaching materials since all students can supposedly read and comprehend the materials at a satisfactory level. If grouping of this kind is undertaken, additional criteria in addition to test data should be considered. These items might include physical aspects, emotional and personality characteristics, educational history and overall level of intelligence. The recommendations of teachers who have had contact with the students in question should be an important consideration. Instructional groups should be constructed on a flexible basis to allow students to enter and depart from the groups as each student's status is studied from time to time.

3. *Evaluation measures can be used to help the teacher of the gifted to purchase and use appropriate instructional materials.* The gifted child at all grade divisions usually reads at an instructional level considerably in excess of his actual grade placement level. A thorough reading evaluation program may provide detailed information regarding the extent of reading acceleration in such vital areas as vocabulary, comprehension, word analysis skills and study skills. This data can be extremely important to educators with regard to the kind and amount of teaching materials purchased. A single text for a given class is rarely, if ever, satisfactory for the gifted student. Therefore, the innovative teacher should provide a wide variety of media materials such as books, journals, tapes, films and specialized sources for use by the able student in accordance with his interests and abilities. The names of suggested materials with their publishers and addresses can be found in the appendices of this volume. Current prices of any given material can be obtained by writing the appropriate publisher.

4. *The data from testing programs can be used effectively in conducting various studies of the students' levels of reading competency.* A careful analysis of test information can be helpful in determining the number of potentially gifted readers in a given class or school. It may be determined that students whose reading achievement test scores are three or more years above grade level are gifted readers and need a different type of instructional program than those who are average or grade level readers. As indicated earlier, these specially designated persons will probably need more challenging material and a more flexible instructional program.

Principles of an Effective Evaluation Program

Any program of reading evaluation for the able or gifted student should have certain characteristics. These are described in the following section.

1. *Numerous kinds of evaluative instruments, both commercial and informal, should be employed.* Some reading competencies such as the nature and depth of reading interests cannot be measured by the usual commercial tests. The upper level norms for these tests are limited in some cases and thus are inadequate for determining the full extent of the reading skill level for the particularly precocious student. Informal tests are usually not suitable for studies since they are without norm information; however, they can be designed to measure such areas as interpretative comprehension which is not included in the usual commercial comprehension tests.

2. *The use of evaluative devices should be on a continuous as well as a periodic basis.* To provide for a current, relevant program of reading instruction, a continuous flow of applicable test data needs to be immediately available. Each teacher instructing gifted children should alter the developmental reading activities to reflect changes in their reading growth in such important areas as vocabulary, comprehension and word analysis.

3. *The testing program undertaken with gifted children should be a unified effort on the part of teachers, administrators, school psychologists, reading specialists and the students themselves.* If the evaluative procedures are to be meaningful for affected

parties, active participation must be encouraged in such important areas as the purposes of the evaluation, names of tests to be administered, scoring procedures and the collection and utilization of data. In too many school settings, the decisions regarding the items just mentioned rest completely with the school principal and resultant misunderstandings occur because there is a lack of communication and general understanding on the part of the student and teacher.

4. *Test results should be explained to each student so he will know what possible implications may be relevant for his present and future educational program.* Since it is hoped that reading skill improvement will not be directed solely by a teacher, each learner needs to know what he can do with respect to self-taught activities which will help him to be a better reader. Older able students often have clearly defined occupational goals in mind which call for specialized reading skills. Self-directed reading activities designed to complement these goals are both useful and practical.

5. *Gifted students at all grade levels should be encouraged to engage in a continuous program of self-appraisal.* They can discover word attack errors by listening to tapes of oral reading exercises. Programmed materials which allow the student to proceed at his own pace are an excellent means of building self appraisal skills. The student also can increase his reading speed by silently reading progressively longer passages in a fixed period of time. He can appraise his present competencies in light of his predetermined future goals. Self-appraisal is one of the most significant evaluation techniques and may have more meaning for the student than the traditional commercial instruments.

6. *Tests should be chosen which measure as closely as possible the stated goals of the reading program which have been established for the able student.* The emphasis of most standardized reading tests appears to be in the general areas of vocabulary and comprehension with little attention given to such matters as word attack, reading speed, reading appreciation and depth of understanding. The use of informal teacher-made evaluative devices designed to uniquely evaluate particular reading objectives

may be the most useful tool for the teacher of the gifted child to employ. Data derived from such tests should provide valuable information to the teacher in the future development of his reading program.

Standardized Reading Tests Available for Gifted Students

There are over one hundred standardized reading tests which can be employed by elementary and secondary teachers for measuring such important reading skills as vocabulary, comprehension, study skills and dictionary skills. Generally speaking all of these instruments can be divided into four different classifications: survey, diagnostic, oral and reading readiness.

Survey (or achievement) tests can be administered to large groups of pupils and characteristically yield a grade placement score in vocabulary and comprehension. Data from these instruments allow the teacher to compare a given student's reading achievement with similar students who constituted the norm groups. Deviations from the norm level also suggest the degree to which a certain student may be retarded or gifted in reading skill development. Those students whose scores deviate two to three grade levels may need an individual diagnostic test if more precise information is needed.

The following is a representative list of survey reading tests which are used at the elementary, junior high and senior high levels:

The Botel Reading Inventory is designed for pupils from Grades 1–12 and evaluates skills in the areas of phonics, general word recognition, reading, listening and word comprehension (Follett).

California Phonics Survey can be administrated to pupils from Grades 7–13 and gives an indication relative to general phonic knowledge (California Test Bureau).

California Reading Test measures basic competencies in vocabulary and comprehension with forms available for use at both the elementary and high school levels (California Test Bureau).

Comprehensive Tests of Basic Skills is designed for Grades 2.5–12 and measures the pupil's ability in general vocabulary and comprehension as well as language and spelling skill areas (California Test Bureau).

Cooperative English Tests: Reading Comprehension is for use with high school students to measure general comprehension, vocabulary and speed and accuracy skills (Educational Testing Service).

Davis Reading Test measures the level and rate of comprehension and can be employed at the high school level (Psychological Corporation).

Diagnostic Reading Tests (Survey Section) can be used with high school and college students to measure rate of reading in addition to general vocabulary and comprehension skills (Committee on Diagnostic Testing).

Gates-MacGinitie Reading Tests have a number of forms for elementary and high school students for measurement of vocabulary comprehension, and speed and accuracy skills (Teachers College Press).

Iowa Every-Pupil Tests of Basic Skills surveys the elementary student's abilities in vocabulary; comprehension; reading maps, graphs, and charts; and skill in the use of specialized sources such as the dictionary and index (Houghton-Mifflin).

Kelley-Greene Reading Comprehension Test is uniquely designed for high school students to evaluate their abilities to retain details and other aspects of the comprehension array (Harcourt, Brace, Jovanovich).

Nelson-Denny Reading Test measures vocabulary, comprehension and rate of reading at the high school level (Houghton-Mifflin).

Sequential Tests of Educational Progress are designed for junior and senior high students and evaluate their ability to comprehend facts, translate ideas and make inferences (Educational Testing Service).

SRA Reading Record evaluates a number of reading skills including reading rate, directory reading, index reading, vocabulary and paragraph comprehension and is intended for use by high school students (Science Research Associates).

For the exceptional child, the use of an individual diagnostic reading test may be useful in determining particular strengths and limitations with regard to overall reading skill development. Many otherwise able students display such limitations as slow reading rate, ineffective comprehension and less than satisfactory vocabulary competencies. Data from diagnostic tests can be used by the teacher to design an instructional program which will challenge the learner to work at his potential level in particular reading skill areas. Three of the most used individual diagnostic tests are described in the next section.

The Diagnostic Reading Scales can be used effectively with elementary school pupils to assess such reading skills as sight-word vocabulary, oral reading, word recognition ability and silent reading comprehension (California Test Bureau).

Durrell Analysis of Reading Difficulty is intended for use with elementary pupils and measures many diverse skills such as oral reading, spelling, handwriting, visual memory, phonics and other forms of word analysis and listening comprehension (Harcourt, Brace, Jovanovich).

Gates-McKillop Reading Diagnostic Test can be administered to elementary and junior high students and evaluates skill areas such as oral reading, spelling, auditory blending, syllabication and auditory discrimination (Teachers College Press).

Oral reading tests can be helpful in providing valuable information relative to a given pupil's word attack skills, interpretative skills and general understanding of the reading passages under consideration. Data obtained from such instruments can be helpful in aiding a pupil to increase reading speed in both oral and silent reading situations. Two of the major oral reading tests are described in the next section.

Gray Oral Reading Test is applicable for both elementary and high school students and yields rate, comprehension and grade equivalent scores along with a diagnostic profile of a student's oral reading errors such as substitutions, omissions and hesitations (Bobbs-Merrill).

Gilmore Oral Reading Test yields a total grade equivalent along with data relating to accuracy and comprehension. Space is allocated for the examiner to make a systematic appraisal of the common oral reading errors such as poor phrasing, monotonous tone, finger pointing and overall expression (Harcourt, Brace, Jovanovich).

Reading readiness tests are employed by many teachers of young children to help them determine if the pupils are ready for formal reading experiences. With the very precocious child, the test could be administered as early as nursery school or kindergarten to assess these factors. Many able pupils know how to read first grade basal reading stories as early as three to four years of age. The results of the readiness tests can help to substantiate or refute the observations of the parent and/or teacher regarding a given child's reading capabilities. Three of the more commonly used readiness tests are discussed in the next section.

The Gates-MacGinitie Readiness Skills Test evaluates the young child's ability to discriminate spoken sounds and visual symbols, follow directions, recognize letters, recognize words and demonstrate visual-motor coordination (Teachers College Press).

The Harrison-Stroud Reading Readiness Test measures such skills as context and auditory clues, auditory discrimination and symbol use (Houghton-Mifflin).

The Metropolitan Readiness Tests consist of subtests which assess a learner's competency in such areas as understanding words, comprehending words and sentences, making number discriminations and demonstrating visual and motor coordination (Harcourt, Brace, Jovanovich).

Principles of Effective Test Administration

Assuming that the correct test has been chosen for a particular child for one or more objectives, a number of practices should be observed if maximum benefit is to be derived from the instrument. Test scores can, in fact, be invalid if the following measures are not observed. Every attempt should be made to insure the proper measure of reading growth; this is especially true when the pupil is thought to be gifted.

1. Careful attention should be given to the length of the testing periods. Generally speaking, tests which consist of several distinct subsections should be administered over a two or three day period. Many pupils have short attention spans and a testing session of one hour in one given day is the maximum time length which should be scheduled.
2. The physical setting of the testing room should be carefully

planned to insure that the room temperature is suitable, proper ventilation is possible and comfortable furniture is available.

3. The test administrator must always be prepared for every phase of the examination process. Time limits, test explanations and scoring processes must be thoroughly understood and observed at all times to insure valid scores.

4. Orientation should be provided for the students so they will know exactly what the purposes of the testing program are. Information should be given relative to how this information will be used to help in the formation of their instructional program.

Summary

There is a number of significant purposes for an evaluation program. An effective plan provides valuable information to the teacher of the gifted child so he can plan a more challenging and motivating reading program.

Numerous standardized instruments of the survey, diagnostic, oral reading and readiness varieties are available for purchase and use by teachers at all grade levels. When these tests are properly chosen and administered according to the principles outlined in this chapter, the teacher will have a valuable body of knowledge about each pupil in his class.

CHAPTER IX

TEACHING PLANS

C AREFUL PLANNING based on diagnosis not only charts the
learning course for a gifted child, but also saves time and
develops his intellectual talents to a higher degree. Planning also
causes the teacher to develop both long range and immediate
goals. These provide direction in learning and aid the development of good scope and sequence in the program.

For the purpose of serving as examples only, sample lesson
plans have been included.

Sample Plans

Plans have been devised for teaching skills in word recognition and comprehension. Possible levels have been indicated,
but these will vary according to individual pupils and their
needs. No time allotment has been suggested for either lesson,
since the creative teacher could delete unnecessary parts or extend sections to provide increased practice or added depth.

Affixes

Middle Elementary Level

I. Purposes
  A. Develop an understanding of affixes as structural clues
     to word recognition.
  B. Use contextual clues to determine the meanings of pre-
     fixes and suffixes. Illustrate with un-, non-, pre-, re-,
     -able, -ible, -some, -ee.
  C. Study the word meaning changes caused by adding
     these affixes.
  D. Apply knowledge of concepts to other words with affixes.

II. Materials
  A. Use sentences on card strips to put as needed in pocket chart.
    1. Jim is kind to animals.
    2. Bill is unkind to animals.
    3. The club party is for members and nonmembers.
    4. Preview the film before showing it to the group.
    5. Your hands are still dirty. Rewash them.
    6. The math problem is workable.
    7. Ants are bothersome on a picnic.
    8. The fireman is an employee of the city.
  B. Use chart of affixes as review

Affix	*Meaning*
un-	(not)
non-	(not)
re-	(back, again)
-able, -ible	(capable of being)
-some	(full of)
-ee	(one who is)

  C. Make root word cards and affix cards (several sets).
    1. Root word examples:

employ	work	hand
train	date	whole
play	view	bother
new	use	group
act	fuse	depend

    2. Affix examples:

un-	inter-	-some
non-	retro-	-ee
pre-	sub-	-less
re-	semi-	-ful
anti-	trans-	-ent
dis-	-able, -ible	-ion

III. Procedure
  A. Introduce the affix concept with un- and non-.
    1. Compare sentences 1 and 2—discuss meanings.
    2. Consider the change in meaning of the root word "member" in sentence 3.

3. Develop the syllable concept.

4. Have children furnish other examples using prefixes (introduce term) un- and non-.

B. Build meanings of pre- and re-.

1. Find the root words in preview and rewash.

2. Develop the syllable concept.

3. How do pre- and re- change the meaning when added to the root words in sentences 4 and 5?

4. Have children furnish other examples.

C. Introduce the term "suffix"—relate it to "prefix."

1. Use sentences 6, 7, and 8 to develop meanings of suffixes and their effects on the meaning of the root words.

2. Develop the syllable concept.

3. Have children furnish other examples.

D. Elicit the generalization of affixes as syllables in words.

E. Review by filling in the simple affix meaning on the chart.

F. Write on the chalkboard examples of root words combined with other affixes to use for applying the concepts learned.

1. Find the syllables.

2. Pronounce the words.

3. Use the words in sentences.

4. Discuss meanings of the root words and new words.

G. Use for independent work.

1. Think of other prefixes and suffixes and try using them in sentences to determine the affix meanings. Make your own chart of affixes and their meanings. Add on to it as you come across new affixes.

2. Use word cards and affix cards to make as many combinations as possible. Determine the meaning changes. Let students make more cards with different affixes.

IV. Evaluation

A. Measure ability to perform without hesitation and with accuracy in both oral and independent work.

B. Evaluate fluency of application of the concepts to new word situations involving affixes.

Comprehension—Character Study

Upper Elementary Level

I. Purposes
   A. Determine the traits of a story character through the clues in the text.
   B. Differentiate between direct statements of the author and inferences drawn by the reader from the material.
   C. Categorize the character description into statements describing physical traits and those showing emotional (personality or disposition) traits.
   D. Use knowledge of traits to make comparisons of characters.
   E. Demonstrate understanding of a character by projecting him (her) into an original situation or story and showing him true to the listed traits.

II. Materials
   A. A story selected for the pupil to read.
   B. Focus on character analysis by use of teacher-made list of suggested questions.
      1. Who was the main character?
      2. Could you describe one physical feature of this character?
      3. How do you know that? Was it stated directly or implied?
      4. What was his (her) role in the story?
      5. How did you feel about him (her)? Why?
      6. Find a statement by the author that justifies your feeling about the character.
      7. Is the statement a direct description of a character trait or does it infer a possible trait?
   C. Use a teacher-made list of descriptive statements about the main character to categorize physical and personality traits into inferred or stated items.
   D. Paper and pencil will be needed.

III. Procedure
   A. Introduce the topic of character study.

1. As an example, select a person known to the child, as the principal, the librarian, the secretary, etc. and have the pupil characterize him (her).
   a. Discuss what is actually known.
   b. Discuss how other traits are inferred by giving specific examples.
2. In what ways in his writing does an author make known the traits—both physical and emotional (personality)—of the characters in his story?
3. Direct descriptions are easy to recognize. Can you think of some ways that are not direct to show traits?

B. Lead into the selected story.
   1. Learn as much as you can about how the main character fits into the plot.
   2. Discover all you can about the physical and emotional traits of the main character.

C. Read the story silently.

D. Discuss the story (pupil and teacher).
   1. Utilize the prepared suggested list of questions.
   2. Explain the assignment for independent work.

E. Use for independent work.
   1. List all you know about the character (stated directly or inferred)—denote those items which are inferred.
   2. Categorize the items as physical or emotional trait descriptions.
   3. Compare the main character to the main character in another story you have read.
   4. Project this character into another situation and write your own brief story depicting the character true to the traits you listed.

IV. Evaluation
   A. Measure the depth of understanding exhibited in pupil-teacher discussion.
   B. Evaluate the insight and depth displayed in completed independent work.
   C. Calculate the application of character analysis to other stories.

APPENDIX A

Book Clubs for Children and Youth

American Education Publications
    Weekly Reader Children's Book Club
    Weekly Reader Family Book Service
    Junior Challenges
    Challenges
    English Paperback Club
The Bookplan
    The Bookplan
E & R Development Company, Inc.
    Hi-Rise Book Club
    Owl Book Club
    Rocket Book Club
    Star Time Book Club
Grolier Reading Program, Inc.
    Beginning Reader's Program
    Companion Library for Boys and Girls
    Dandelion Library
The Junior Discoverers Book Club
    The Junior Discoverers Book Club
Junior Literary Guild
Division of Doubleday and Company
    Junior Literary Guild
    Young Adults
Nelson Doubleday, Inc.
    Best-in-Children's Books
    Junior Deluxe Editions Club
    Young World Reader's Club
Parents' Magazine Enterprises, Inc.
    Read Aloud and Easy Reading Program
Scholastic Book Services

Arrow Book Club	4–6
Campus Book Club	10–12
Lucky Book Club	2–3
See-Saw Book Program	K–1
Teen Age Book Club	7–9

Wisconsin Book Club, Inc.
Wisconsin Book Club
Young Readers Press, Inc.
Best Loved Girls' Books
Young Readers

To obtain further information about children's book clubs, contact the following sources:

American Library Association
50 East Huron St.
Chicago, Illinois   60611

Children's Book Center
University of Chicago
Graduate Library School
Chicago, Illinois   60637

Children's Book Council
175 Fifth Avenue
New York, N. Y.   10010

Irvin Hass
Book Club Consultants
65 Diana's Trail
Roslyn Estates, New York   11576

APPENDIX B

Periodicals Suitable for Gifted Children

AMERICAN GIRL (Girl Scouts of the USA)
This journal is the official Girl Scout magazine of interest to pre-teen and teen-age girls.
AMERICAN HERITAGE: THE MAGAZINE OF HISTORY (American Heritage Publishing Company)
A wide coverage of Americana is presented in this hard-cover periodical. There are many illustrations.
AMERICAN RED CROSS YOUTH JOURNAL (American National Red Cross)

This periodical is an interesting source of social studies information with an emphasis on current social problems.

AMERICAN RED CROSS YOUTH NEWS (American National Red Cross)

The publication is a useful little magazine with articles related to the elementary curriculum. There is a section of material contributed by readers.

AMERICAN SCHOLAR: A QUARTERLY FOR THE INDE-PENDENT THINKER (United Chapters of Phi Beta Kappa)

This is a scholarly, but not pedantic magazine covering such topics as world politics and contemporary society.

AMERICAN SCIENTIST (Society of the Sigma Xi)

This is a technical and well-documented science journal with a wide range of topics with appeal for the advanced high school student.

ANIMAL KINGDOM (New York Zoological Society)

Information about animals throughout the world is covered in this small publication.

ANNALS OF THE AMERICAN ACADEMY OF POLITICAL AND SOCIAL SCIENCE (American Political Science Association)

Each issue contains a discussion of a single topic from all aspects, allowing the reader to draw his own conclusions.

ANTIOCH REVIEW (Antioch Press)

This university literary publication contains fiction poetry and essays which would appeal to the gifted student. Of special interest would be the book review section.

ART AND MAN (Scholastic Book Services)

The publication is more of a study unit than a magazine as it covers a theme represented and developed through works of art and designed mainly for classroom use. Recordings, slides and filmstrips are available.

ATLANTIC MONTHLY (Atlantic Monthly)

Although mainly considered to be a literary magazine, this periodical also covers material on economics, sociology and current issues.

ATLAS: BEST FROM THE WORLD PRESS (Atlas: Best from the World Press)

This magazine presents the world news of the past month. It gives students an opportunity to see global news from another viewpoint.

AUDUBON (National Audubon Society)

This periodical features spectacular photographs which help to foster an appreciation for wildlife, natural resources and natural beauty.

BLACK WORLD (Johnson Publishing Co.)

This journal contains several articles about one subject. Each article is documented and has reference value as well as reading interest.

BOY'S LIFE (Boy Scouts of America)

This magazine designed for boys ages 8–14 is full of interesting articles dealing with sports, nature, history, hobbies and camping.

BUSINESS WEEK (McGraw-Hill, Inc.)

The world of business is covered in this thorough weekly report.

CHILD LIFE (Review Publishing Company)

Story Time, Feature Time, and Play Time are three main features found in this well-known children's magazine.

CHILDREN'S DIGEST (Parent's Magazine Enterprises, Inc.)

This is a digest size collection of stories, articles and activities for ages 7–12.

CHILDREN'S PLAYMATE (Review Publishing Company)

This is a collection of stories, poems, puzzles, riddles and activities for ages 3–8.

CO-ED (Scholastic Book Services)

A wide variety of early teen-age interests are presented in this magazine.

CONGRESSIONAL DIGEST: AN INDEPENDENT MONTHLY FEATURING CONTROVERSIES IN CONGRESS (Congressional Digest Corporation)

As the title states, this digest presents both sides of current issues in Congress. It could be useful for speech and debate courses.

CONGRESSIONAL QUARTERLY SERVICE (Congressional Quarterly, Inc.)

This service includes the CQ WEEKLY REPORT which analyzes current congressional activities, the QUARTERLY CUMULATIVE INDEX, and the CQ ALMANAC which digest the material in the weekly reports.

CRISIS: A RECORD OF THE DARK RACES (Crisis: A Record of the Dark Races)

This official publication of the NAACP covers social and political problems involving blacks.

ENVIRONMENTAL ACTION (Environmental Action, Inc.)

This magazine was the newsletter for "Environmental Teach-In" which was responsible for Earth Day in 1970. It now speaks directly to young people who are concerned about environmental control.

EXPLORING (Boy Scouts of America)

This is a promising magazine for both boys and girls edited and written by young people.

FOCUS (American Geographical Society)

Each issue concentrates on a region, country or resource and discusses historical influences and interaction of physical, social, and economic factors.

HIGHLIGHTS FOR CHILDREN (Highlights for Children)

A variety of excellent material for children age 3–12 can be found in this outstanding magazine.

HORIZON (American Heritage Publishing Company)

Art, literature, philosophy, music and history are covered in the hard-covered periodical of the humanities.

HUMPTY-DUMPTY'S MAGAZINE: A MAGAZINE FOR LITTLE CHILDREN (Parent's Magazine Enterprises, Inc.)

This publication is for the beginning reader up to age 7.

INGENUE (Dell Publishing Company)

This magazine caters to the typical interests of the pre-teen girl.

JACK AND JILL (Saturday Evening Post Company)

This fine magazine for children up to grade 5 contains stories, articles, things to do and original writings by readers.

JUNIOR SCHOLASTIC: A NATIONAL MAGAZINE FOR JUNIOR HIGH SCHOOL AND UPPER ELEMENTARY GRADES (Scholastic Book Services)

This current events weekly is designed for classroom use.

KIDS (Kids)

This is a special magazine for kids by kids themselves. The magazine features stories, poems, cartoons and biographies.

LITERARY CAVALCADE (Scholastic Book Service)

This is a literary magazine for young adults including fiction and a full-length play. Information on college selection is also included.

NATION (Nation Associates, Inc.)

This is a journal of critical international and national opinions. It should provide stimulating reading for the mature reader.

NATIONAL GEOGRAPHIC MAGAZINE (National Geographic Society)

An interesting coverage of geography and travel is presented in this magazine. Outstanding pictures and maps provide enrichment for all levels.

NATIONAL GEOGRAPHIC SCHOOL BULLETIN (National Geographic Society)

This leaflet features geography and natural science articles and is designed for enrichment in the elementary school.

NATIONAL OBSERVER (National Observer)

This is an informative periodical in newspaper form featuring news coverage and reviews.

NATIONAL WILDLIFE: DEDICATED TO THE USE OF OUR NATURAL RESOURCES (National Wild Life Federation)

This is a colorful publication which features articles on outdoor recreation, endangered species, federal and state parks and forests and ecology.

NATURAL HISTORY (American Museum of Natural History)

This magazine includes a wide range of highly informative articles on the natural sciences with emphasis on conservation, anthropology and astrology.

NEWSWEEK (Newsweek Subscription Service)

This well-known weekly magazine covers the news of the past week.

PLAYS: THE DRAMA MAGAZINE (Plays, Inc.)

Plays on all levels are included in this magazine, and can be presented by subscribers without royalty fees.

RANGER RICK'S NATURE MAGAZINE (National Wildlife Federation)

Animals, plants, natural history, science, conservation, nature crafts and games are all featured in this colorful and informative magazine.

READ MAGAZINE (American Educational Publications)

This is a classroom magazine which contains specific reading skills and a special section for original work by students.

READERS AND WRITERS (Readers and Writers)

This magazine is aimed at developing writers with the main audience being creative writing classes.

SATURDAY REVIEW (Saturday Review, Inc.)

This magazine has now become a review of the arts, society, education and the sciences.

SCHOLASTIC NEWS SERIES (Scholastic Book Services)

News Pilot	— 1	
News Ranger	— 2	
News Trails	— 3	
New Explorer	— 4	
Young Citizen	— 5	
News Time	— 6	
Vacation Fun	2–3	(Summer)
Merry-Go-Round	4–5	(Summer)
Summer Time	6	(Summer)

SCHOLASTIC VOICE (Scholastic Book Services)

This magazine is primarily concerned with language and communication.

SENIOR SCHOLASTIC

JUNIOR SCHOLASTIC (Scholastic Book Services)

These classroom magazines are designed for the average and above average students.

SESAME STREET MAGAZINE (Sesame Street Magazine)

This colorful magazine for the pre-reader is based on ideas from the highly successful T.V. program.

SEVENTEEN (Seventeen Subscription Dept.)

This is a browsing magazine for the teen-age girl.

TIME (Time, Inc.)

This weekly news magazine covers not only the news but also the arts and sciences.

TRAVEL (Travel Magazine, Inc.)

This magazine provides enrichment for pupil study of the geography of America and other countries. It also has articles on art, food, literature and social studies pertaining to the various countries.

U. S. NEWS & WORLD REPORT (U. S. News & World Report)

Extensive reporting of recent news events along with appropriate comment is included in this popular news weekly.

APPENDIX C

Annotated Booklist for Teachers

Barbe, Walter Burke: *Psychology and Education of the Gifted: Selected Readings.* New York, Appleton-Century-Crofts, 1965.

A variety of articles on the gifted is contained in this fine volume.

Beck, Joan: *How to Raise a Brighter Child.* New York, Trident Press, 1967.

Although this book was designed to show parents how to provide a stimulating environment for their pre-school children, teachers can also benefit from much of the information.

Bond, Guy L. and Tinker, Miles A.: *Reading Difficulties: Their Diagnosis and Correction,* 2nd ed. New York, Appleton-Century-Crofts, 1967.

Although this book is aimed at the remedial teacher, it contains good basic information for reading teachers on any level.

Bricklin, Barry and Bricklin, Patricia M.: *Bright Child—Poor Grades.* New York, Dell, 1967.

The causes of failure and underachievement among intelligent children are discussed in this penetrating study. The book is divided into two sections. The first section details the psychological reasons for failure, and the second section gives positive recommendations.

Bridges, S. A., ed.: *Gifted Children and the Brentwood Experiment.* London, Sir Isaac Pitman and Sons Ltd., 1969.

This report tells of the work with the gifted at Brentwood's College of Education in England. It is designed to help teachers who are aware that they have superior children in their classes but who are unsure of how to deal with them.

Carlsen, G. Robert: *Books and the Teen-Age Reader.* New York, Harper and Row, 1967.

All areas of teen-age reading are examined in this book. The annotated bibliographies and guides to reference books are most beneficial.

Cohen, Joseph W.: *The Superior Student in American Higher Education.* New York, McGraw-Hill, 1966.

This is a collection of papers dealing with honors programs in colleges and universities.

Cushenbery, Donald C.: *Reading Improvement in the Elementary School.* West Nyack, N. Y., Parker, 1969.

This concise book presents practical suggestions to assist the classroom teacher with the teaching of reading.

Cushenbery, Donald C.: *Remedial Reading in the Secondary School.* West Nyack, Parker, 1972.

This is a very useful and comprehensive guide for all teachers in the secondary school. Many specific suggestions are presented.

Dickinson, Rita Mitton: *Caring for the Gifted.* North Quincy, Christopher, 1970.

Good, useable information is presented in this book and is directed to parents, teachers and to the gifted themselves.

Duker, Sam: *Individualized Reading: An Annotated Bibliography.* Metuchen, Scarecrow, 1968.

All areas and phases of individualized reading are covered in these complete yet concise bibliographies.

Durkin, Dolores: *Teaching Them to Read.* Boston, Allyn & Bacon, 1970.

This text outlines a total reading program and tells what a student must know to be a better reader.

Engelmann, Siegfried and Engelmann, Therese: *Give Your Child a Superior Mind: A Program for the Pre-School Child.* New York, Simon & Schuster, 1966.

This programmed guide is designed for parents. It gives explicit instruction and information on how to develop the intellect of the pre-school child. Elementary teachers can benefit from this book also.

Fallon, Berlie J. and Filgo, Dorothy J.: *Forty States Innovate to Improve School Reading Programs.* Bloomington, Indiana, Phi Delta Kappa, 1970.

Seventy-five exemplary programs ranging from the readiness level through the high school level are described in this volume.

Farr, Roger: *Measurement and Evaluation of Reading.* New York, Harcourt, Brace and Jovanovich, 1970.

Essays concerning measurement and evaluation techniques are combined in this book.

Fine, Benjamin: *Underachievers: How Can They Be Helped?* New York, E. P. Dutton, 1967.

This presents a broad look at the problem of underachievement with several examples of what is being done to remedy the situation.

Gallagher, James J.: *Teaching Gifted Students: A Book of Readings.* Boston, Allyn & Bacon, 1965.

Special teaching methods, new curriculum movements and the classroom environment as it pertains to the gifted are some of the topics discussed in this collection of articles.

Gallagher, James J., Aschner, Mary Jane and Jenne', William: *Productive Thinking of Gifted Children in Classroom Interaction.* Washington, D. C., CEC Research Monograph, Series B, #B-5, 1967.

This is an in-depth research study recording various thought processes of the gifted student in the classroom. The study then attempts to show various attitudes and relations of the gifted in the classroom as based on this recorded information.

Gold, Milton J.: *Education of the Intellectually Gifted.* Columbus, Ohio, Charles E. Merrill Books, Inc., 1965.

This is a complete text about the gifted. It includes information on the identification of the gifted, programs for the gifted, guidance for the gifted and even information on selection of teachers for the gifted.

Grost, Audrey: *Genius in Residence.* Englewood Cliffs, N. J., Prentice-Hall, 1970.

This interesting account of the family and school life of a

gifted child as told by his mother asks pertinent questions about whether American education is meeting all the needs in the wide range of student abilities.

Guilford, J. P., *The Nature of Human Intelligence.* New York, McGraw-Hill, 1967.

A very thorough discussion and explanation of the basic factors in intelligence are presented in this volume.

Harris, Albert J.: *How to Increase Reading Ability,* 5th ed. New York, McKay, 1970.

This updated edition by Harris continues to present a guide for dealing with children who are reading below their expectancy.

Heilman, Arthur W.: *Principles and Practices of Teaching Reading,* 2nd ed. Columbus, Charles E. Merrill, 1967.

Individualized reading and linguistics are among the new developments discussed in this text.

Henderson, Richard L. and Green, Donald Ross: *Reading for Meaning in the Elementary School.* Englewood Cliffs, Prentice-Hall, 1969.

The reading process is explored in this fine primary source for pre-service and in-service teachers.

Hildreth, Gertrude H.: *Introduction to the Gifted.* New York, McGraw-Hill, 1969.

Originating from the author's personal experiences, this complete text is designed for use in education and psychology classes concerned with the exceptional child.

Jones, Reginald L.: *Problems and Issues in the Education of Exceptional Children.* Boston, Houghton Mifflin, 1971.

This is a collection of writings dealing with issues and problems in the psychology and education of the gifted and other exceptional children.

Karlin, Robert: *Teaching Elementary Reading Principles and Strategies.* New York, Harcourt, Brace and Jovanovich, 1971.

The author believes that teachers must understand the rationale underlying various reading methods. Insights into some of the problem areas in reading are presented, and ways of improving the teaching of reading are shown.

Kirk, Samuel A.: *Educating Exceptional Children.* Boston, Houghton Mifflin, 1972.

There is an excellent chapter on the gifted in this text on exceptional children. An interesting feature is a brief comment about the gifted throughout history.

Leedy, Paul D.: *A Key to Better Reading*. New York, McGraw-Hill, 1968.

Methods for improving such reading skills as critical reading of magazines or newspapers are presented by Leedy for the advanced reader.

Logan, Virgil: Logan, Lillian and Patterson, Lorena: *Creative Communication: Teaching the Language Arts*. New York, McGraw-Hill, 1973.

This text focuses on creative communication and how creativity is involved in each of the language arts.

Love, Harold D.: *Educating Exceptional Children in Regular Classrooms*. Springfield, Charles C Thomas, 1972.

This author presents the view that exceptional children can be educated in the regular classroom. An informative chapter on the gifted is included.

Love, Harold D.: *Exceptional Children in a Modern Society*. Dubuque, William C. Brown, 1967.

This is a unified book on exceptional children with an excellent chapter on the gifted. The gifted child is identified and major trends and issues are discussed.

Martinson, Ruth A.: *Curriculum Enrichment for the Gifted in the Primary Grades*. Englewood Cliffs, Prenctice-Hall, 1968.

The purpose of this book is to help teachers of young elementary children plan for their gifted students. Many practical suggestions and examples are given for meeting special interests and needs, questioning effectively and choosing auxiliary resources.

Moore, George N. and Woodruff, G. Willard: *Providing for Children's Differences*. Wellesley, Curriculum Associates, 1970.

Teachers seeking better use of learning time, space and materials, and who wish to improve the child's school environment and meet demands of curriculum will find this a particularly helpful book.

Olson, Arthur V. and Ames, Wilbur S.: *Teaching Reading Skills in Secondary Schools*. Scranton, International Textbook, 1970.

This book discusses the teaching of reading skills in the high school. It covers reading skills in the content areas and explores ways to develop vocabulary and word recognition skills.

Philadelphia Suburban School Study Council, Group A: *Improving Programs for the Gifted.* Danville, Interstate, 1965.

This report discusses the philosophy, goals and problems of a program for the gifted. Many specific examples for fostering creativity are presented for all subject areas from kindergarten through senior high.

Pines, Maya: *Revolution in Learning: The Years from Birth to Six.* New York, Harper and Row, 1967.

This is a general discussion of developments in early childhood education based on the studies of such noted persons as Piaget, Hunt and Jerome Bruner. The talking typewriter, Operation Headstart and early reading are among ideas and programs examined.

Plowman, Paul D. and Rice, Joseph P.: *California Project Talent.* Sacramento, California State Department of Education, 1967.

Education programs for the gifted in California are examined in this volume.

Raph, Jane Beasley; Goldberg, Miriam L.; and Passow, Harry A.: *Bright Underachievers: Studies of Scholastic Underachievement Among Intellectually Superior High School Students.* New York, Teachers College Press, 1966.

This book studies the behaviors and feeling of intellectually superior high school underachievers as well as the remedial procedures used with them. The book contains a large section which reviews the literature concerning gifted underachievers.

Rice, Joseph P.: *The Gifted: Developing Total Talent.* Springfield, Charles C Thomas, 1970.

This book is written for teachers, parents, counselors and administrators. It broadly views the education of the gifted from academic and professional preparations to athletic, technical and performing art skills.

Rucker, Chauncy N. and Rabinstein, eds.: *Exceptional Children: An Introduction.* New York, MSS. Educational Publishing, 1969.

Readings dealing with the gifted and other exceptional children are collected in this volume.

Schubert, Delwyn and Torgerson, Theodore L.: *Improving Reading in the Elementary School.* Dubuque, Brown, 1968.

This book discusses individualized instruction in reading. It also looks into word recognition and word analysis difficulties. A very helpful appendix is included.

Sharp, Evelyn: *Thinking is Child's Play*. New York, E. P. Dutton, 1969.

The first part of this book discusses how young children learn to think as theorized by well-known psychologists, and the second portion contains games which aid in teaching logical thinking to young children.

Smith, James A.: *Creative Teaching of Reading and Literature in the Elementary School*. Boston, Allyn and Bacon, 1967.

This book is the third of seven in a series on creative teaching. It presents an exciting and positive approach to teaching the basic issues in reading and offers challenging methods for teaching literature and poetry.

Stauffer, Russell G.: *The Language Experience Approach to the Teaching of Reading*. New York, Harper and Row, 1970.

This source presents a method for developing sequential skills through the language experience approach.

Thomas, George I. and Crescimbeni, Joseph: *Guiding the Gifted Child*. New York, Random House, 1966.

This book suggests a variety of identification techniques other than intelligence tests to use in recognizing the gifted student. Alternate methods of meeting the needs of the gifted are examined such as special classes, acceleration, enrichment and special programs and activities.

Tinker, Miles A.: *Bases for Effective Reading*. Minneapolis, University of Minnesota Press, 1965.

This five-part text discusses various methods for teaching effective reading.

Torrence, Paul E.: *Gifted Children in the Classroom*. New York, Macmillan, 1965.

This book contains ideas on ways to develop creative reading ability and improve research skills. It also discusses the nature, identification and development of gifted children. A variety of curriculum provisions is discussed.

Wallach, Michael A. and Wings, Cliff W.: *The Talented Student: A Validation of the Creative—Intelligence Distinction*. New York, Holt, Rinehart and Winston, 1969.

These authors view IQ scores as less reliable predictors of success than extracurricular accomplishments. The book is directed not only to educators and psychologists in general, but in particular to those who select students as candidates for graduate schools and for financial aid.

Wallen, Carl J.: *Word Attack Skills in Reading.* Columbus, Charles E. Merrill, 1969.

A special process for teaching word attack skills is presented with illustrated lessons to help the teacher adopt these ideas for use in the classroom.

Witty, Paul A., ed.: *Reading for the Gifted and the Creative Student.* Newark, International Reading Association, 1971.

This publication discusses the position of the gifted in education today and presents several innovative programs. It also characterizes the gifted child and defines the role of the parent and teacher.

Witty, Paul Andrew; Freeland, Alma Moore; and Grotberg, Edith H.: *The Teaching of Reading: A Developmental Process.* Boston, D. C. Heath, 1966.

Although this book is basically a developmental text, it does give some special attention to challenging the superior and gifted student.

APPENDIX D

Instructional Materials for the Gifted

Publisher	Title	Description
Baldridge Reading Instruction Materials	Brim Student's Kit Jr. High—College	A boxed kit of instructional materials to be used in teaching reading and study skills related to the content areas.
Baldridge Reading Instruction Materials	Brim Teacher's Manual	A complete guide to implementing materials in the Brim Student's Kit.
Barnell Loft	Specific Skills Series	Contains exercises in eight different skill areas: Following Directions, Using the Context,

Publisher	*Title*	*Description*
		Getting the Facts, Locating the Answer, Working with Sounds, Getting the Main Idea, Drawing Conclusions, and Detecting Sequence. The materials are written at six different reading levels.
Benefic Press	Animal Adventure Series Primary	Warm, humorous adventures of animals in their natural environment.
Benefic Press	Moonbeam Series Primary	Stimulates a child's interest in reading. Real-life experiences, fast paced action, together with anecdotal humor.
Benefic Press	World of Adventure Primary	Combines fact, fiction, and fun to stimulate the enthusiasm and kindle the imagination of the young reader.
Benefic Press	House of Books	A multi-level, individualized reading program offering a variety of subjects and titles at specific reading levels from Pre-primer I— Grade 6.
Benefic Press	Thinking Box 5–9	Provides specific guidance and procedures combined with content for the development of critical thinking skills.
Bobbs-Merrill	Childhood of Famous Americans Series	Biographies of over one hundred famous Americans written at middle grade levels for interest levels through junior high.
Bowmar	What Is ———? Primary	A set of six books designed to develop concepts of shape, distance and size.

Publisher	Title	Description
Bowmar	Children Writing Research Reports Intermediate	A kit of curriculum materials that provides a simple, rational structure emphasizing clear thinking and purposeful organization for the written and oral presentation of non-fiction material.
Bowmar	Explorers 3	Dramatic biographies of exploration, discovery, and conquest are included in these books.
Bowmar	Holidays 1–2	Stories are about celebrations in America and other lands.
Bowmar	American Democracy 3	Books deal with our national symbols, their history and how they relate to our nation and ideals.
Bowmar	How They Lived 3	Vivid documentaries of America's growth and heritage.
Bowmar	Living in Today's World 3	Timely books to enrich studies of countries and cultures.
Bowmar	Science 3	Simple explanations of physical and natural sciences.
Bowmar	Defenders of Freedom 4	Stirring biographies of military men in action.
Bowmar	Creative People in the Arts and Sciences 4	Life stories of the world's creative geniuses.
Bowmar	Rivers 4	Stories of the great rivers and the cultures they have influenced.
Bowmar	Toward Freedom 4	History and heritage of black Americans are revealed in these books
Bowmar	Wonder of Wonders: Man	The story of man, his human physiology and sociological implications.

Publisher	Title	Description
Bowmar	Reading as Thinking: Paragraph Comprehension Secondary	Two books designed to upgrade reading potential of college-bound students.
Bowmar	Organization Skills Intermediate	
Curriculum Associates	Sequences and Exercises Primary	Emphasis in these materials is on activities that introduce, review, practice and reinforce.
Curriculum Associates	A Child-Centered Language Arts Program Intermediate	Focus of this program is on the development of each child's unique creative ability in oral and written expression. The program starts with simple tasks based on observation, memory and elementary descriptive skills, then builds toward those requiring analysis of data.
Curriculum Associates	Language Arts Sampler K–8	A program designed to allow children to work at their own level and proceed at their own rate; concentrates on vocabulary growth and creative writing.
Curriculum Associates	Thirty Lessons in Outlining Elementary Advanced	These lessons help children understand and prepare outlines.
Educators' Publishing Service	A Vocabulary Builder Series 6–12	A vocabulary building series of seven volumes developed for use in grades six through twelve. At each level, a basic vocabulary list is used in comprehensive drills of meaning, pronunciation and spelling.
Fearon Publishers	Adventures in Space	A series of books containing short stories

Publisher	Title	Description
		which draws on the student's "television knowledge." There are three books in each of the four sets in the series.
Field Publications	Leonard Equals Einstein Leonard Discovers Africa Primary	Fantasy
Field Publications	Jim Forest and The Flood Jim Forest and The Lone Wolf Gulch Primary	Social Studies & Conservation
Field Publications	Gatie the Alligator Sleeky the Otter Skippy the Dolphin Tawny the Mountain Lion Bounder the Jackrabbit Thar the Mouse Ruff the Wolf Arctas the Grizzly Primary	Natural Science
Field Publications	Frogmen & Action Danger Below Whale Hunt Rocket Divers Primary	Oceanography
Field Publications	Mystery of Morgan Castle Mystery of Marble Angel Primary	Mystery
Follett	Just Beginning to Read Books	These stories are for children with a small preprimer vocabulary who have been learning to read for about 6–8 weeks.
Follett	Beginning to Read	These books will instill enthusiasm for reading and a feeling of accomplishment in even the youngest reader.

Publisher	*Title*	*Description*
Garrard	Reading Shelf K–4	These books can be built into a delightfully interesting and different supplemental or individualized reading program.
Garrard	Discovery 1–2	Short, introductory biographies for the primary grades.
Garrard	Indians 1–2	Rich cultural heritage is highlighted in these action-filled biographies.
Garrard	Americans All 3	Biographies of great Americans of all races, creeds and national origins are featured in these books.
Garrard	Colony Leaders 3	Biographies which emphasize the roles played by founders of America.
Garrard	Sports 3	Include histories of individual sports as well as biographies of great names in sports.
Garrard	Century 4–5	Biographies of the makers of world history.
Ginn	Ginn Enrichment Readers 1–6	Books expand reading experiences and kindle new interests.
C. S. Hammond	Words Are Important	Series is designed for grade levels 7–college and emphasizes word study and vocabulary improvement.
Harcourt Brace Jovanovich, Inc.	Phonics Practice Program	A largely self-teaching program presented on durable cards listing groups of phonograms accompanied by a picture clue which relates to one of the words. Contains 259 illustrated phonics practice cards, and teacher's guide in storage box.

Publisher	Title	Description
Harcourt Brace Jovanovich, Inc.	Adventures in Literature 7–12	A soundly organized collection of literature and study aids with a fine arts program that enriches the literature.
Harcourt Brace Jovanovich, Inc.	Adventures in Good Books Series 7–12	Series enriches the study of literature for students in grades 7–12.
Harcourt Brace Jovanovich, Inc.	Let's Enjoy Poetry I & II Book I—Primary Book II—Intermediate	Two anthologies containing over 400 selected poems together with suggestions for presentation should aid the teacher in selling poetry.
Harcourt Brace Jovanovich, Inc.	Tales From the Four Winds Levels 6–12 The Golden Goose and Other Plays 6–9	A collection of some of the world's favorite stories, presented as plays, provides exercise in interpretative oral reading.
Harcourt Brace Jovanovich, Inc.	The Straw Ox and Other Plays 8–10 The Bag of Fire and Other Plays 10–12	
Harcourt Brace Jovanovich, Inc.	The Crowded House and Other Plays 11–12	
Harcourt Brace Jovanovich, Inc.	Discoveries Intermediate	A well-designed individualized approach to reading designed to develop reading skills making use of group as well as individual readers' skills, worktexts and storycards. Prepared by the Bank Street College of Education.
Harcourt Brace Jovanovich, Inc.	Merit Books Intermediate	A series of popular full-length juvenile books on a variety of subjects in a broad range of reading

Publisher	*Title*	*Description*
		levels designed to promote independent reading.
Harcourt Brace Jovanovich, Inc.	The New Riverside Literature Series	Series offers a broad selection of classics, traditional and modern.
Harcourt Brace Jovanovich, Inc.	Literature: Uses of the Imagination Secondary Wish and Nightmare Circle of Stories Jr. High	A paperback program presenting world literature in thematic units.
Harcourt Brace Jovanovich, Inc.	Design for Good Reading	A four-level developmental reading program for the high school designed to improve skills, comprehension and creative-critical reading ability.
Harper & Row, Publishers	I Can Read Books K–3 Grown Up Occupations I Can Read History Books Little Bear Books I Can Read Mystery Books Sports I Can Read Books	Creative stories written and illustrated for the beginning reader.
Harper & Row, Publishers	The Creative Reading Program Levels 1–12	An enrichment series which stresses the development of positive attitudes toward literature. Paperback editions of popular children's stories are accompanied at each of four levels by filmstrips and recordings.
Harper & Row, Publishers	Patterns in Design for Reading Freeways to Reading: Literature Levels 3–8 Freeways to Reading:	Six boxed sets of books including selections from literature and content specialties designed to encourage desire to read independently.

Publisher	Title	Description

	Literature
	    Levels 9–10
	Freeways to Reading:
	Literature
	    Levels 11–12	

Harper &
Row,
Publishers
	Freeways to Reading:
	Science & Social Studies
	    Levels 3–12
	Freeways to Reading:
	Literature
	    Levels 13–18
	Freeways to Reading:
	Science & Social Studies
	    Levels 13–18	

D. C. Heath	Guide to Effective Reading Secondary	Self-teaching workbook which emphasizes skill development in such areas as speed, flexibility, decoding skills, meaning vocabulary, dictionary usage, study skills, skimming, organization skills, etc.; for the college-bound student.
Hoffman Information Systems, Inc.	"Gold Series" Reading Achievement Units	Structured reading materials composed of six units of grade levels 3–9. Each of the six units is composed of ten albums each including four film strips and two records on a wide variety of subjects.
Holt, Rinehart and Winston	Instant Readers	Books are written for the developing student and have strong eye and ear appeal. Stories are based upon familiar cultural sequences and use picture clues and repetition of phrases to aid students in independent reading.
Houghton Mifflin	Piper Books Intermediate	Carefully researched authentic biographies of great men and women of the past.

Publisher	Title	Description
Learn, Incorporated	Communication Through Effective Reading	Unit consists of a teacher's guide and student packs designed to encourage individual progress in skill development.
Lyons and Carnahan	The Curriculum Enrichment Series Primer–6	A series of enrichment books designed for the more able readers who need additional challenge.
Mafex Associates, Inc.	Book I—Spur-On 3–7	Independent, self-teaching research projects for enrichment.
McCormick-Mathers	New Dimensions in Literature 9–12	A flexible, multi-volume literature program leading to improvement and enrichment in reading, listening, speaking and writing skills.
McGraw Hill Book Company, Webster Division	American Language Today	Elementary language series based on linguistic concepts which is designed to promote active student involvement in developing language skills.
Charles E. Merrill Books, Inc.	Merrill Reading Skill-texts 1–6	A series of text-work-books designed to build all reading skills that can be used to supplement any basal reading series.
Charles E. Merrill Books, Inc.	Merrill Reading Skill-tapes	Cassette tapes to accompany the Skill-texts permit students to work individually and independently. Tapes introduce selected stories, pose questions, read the story and present follow-up activities.
New Dimensions in Education,	The Name of the Game 6–12	Junior high-senior high language arts program

Publisher	*Title*	*Description*
Inc.		utilizing materials that focus on real life problems. Includes paperback collection, records and game. Reading levels 5–8.
Noble & Noble	Story-Go-Round	Sixteen popular children's books with correlated cassettes offer the young child listening and reading experiences designed to develop enthusiasm for reading and confidence in exploring literature.
Odyssey Press, Bobbs-Merrill Company	The Odyssey Reader: Ideas on Style A Handbook to Literature The Questing Mind Thought in English Prose Understanding the Essay	Textbooks for honors and advanced placement classes.
Perma Bound, Hertzberg-New Method, Inc.	This company offers collections of paperback books such as the following: Black Literature 9–12 "The Play is The Thing" 9–12 Film Making and Film Techniques 10–12 In Search of Identity 9–12	
Prentice Hall	Be a Better Reader Series 4–12	Major emphasis in this collection of books is in the area of word attack and vocabulary in the content areas of social studies, literature, biological science and mathematics.

Publisher	*Title*	*Description*
Prentice Hall	One to One—Junior Edition 　Primary One to One 　Intermediate	Individualized Reading Programs.
Pyramid Books	Arena Books Fabric of our Times	Collections of books for supplemental reading.
Random House	Landmark Books 　Intermediate	Books should appeal to students who enjoy reading about historical events and important people.
Random House	Reaching Higher 　3 Reaching Forward 　4	
Random House	Reaching Ahead 　5 Reaching Beyond 　6	
Scholastic Book Services	Pattern for Reading 　8–12 Scholastic Literature Units 　6–11	Self help reading improvement text. These units include books for individual reading to challenge advanced readers.
Science Research Associates	The Dimensions Series 　4–12 　Countries and Cultures 　5–9 　We are Black 　4–8	A series designed to stimulate interest in independent reading by offering progressively more challenging material.
Science Research Associates	An American Album 　4–8 Manpower and Natural Resources 　8–12	
Science Research Associates	Survey of Reading/Study Efficiency 　9–college	Gives students an insight into their own reading and study habits.
Scott Foresman & Co.	The Bright Horizons Program 　1–6	This is a program designed to develop critical reading skills of children reading a year or more above grade level.

Publisher	Title	Description
Scott Foresman & Co.	The Wide Horizons Readers 1–6 In Other Words I . . . A Beginning Thesaurus 3–4	
Scott Foresman & Co.	In Other Words II . . . A Junior Thesaurus 5–6	
Scott Foresman & Co.	The following collections are suitable for average and above-average students:	
Scott Foresman & Co.	America Reads Program (Literature) –7–8 Projection Counterpoint	
Scott Foresman & Co.	Basic Reading Program –7–8 Dimensions Challenges	
Scott Foresman & Co.	Three Chronologies of Literature—9–12 The American Tradition The Early Development of English Literature Three Centuries of English Literature	
Scott Foresman & Co.	Collections of Novelettes —9–12 Edges of Reality The Fractured Image The Life Force	
Scott Foresman & Co.	Scott Foresman Reading Systems Invitations to Personal Reading Primary	A component to be used for enrichment.
Simon & Schuster	English Language Skill Books: Secondary Faster Reading Self-Taught	

Publisher	Title	Description
	30 Days to a More Powerful Vocabulary Word Power Made Easy	
L. W. Singer	The Carousel Book Program Primary	A program of individualized reading activities for application, enrichment and appreciation.
Teachers College Press	Gates-Peardon Reading Exercises Intro. A-B, Gr. 1 Preparatory A-B, Gr. 2 Elementary, Gr. 3 Intermediate, Gr. 4 Advanced, Gr. 5	Booklets are designed to build and strengthen reading skills in the elementary grades. They deal with understanding the main idea of a story, remembering details and following directions.
Webster Division, McGraw Hill Book Company	Webster Classroom Reading Clinic	Components in this laboratory aid elementary children in building skills in comprehension, sight word vocabulary and phonics. Included in the kit are 224 reading skill cards with questions, twenty copies of Conquests in Reading and The Magic World of Dr. Spello.
Webster Publishing Company, Inc.	Adventures in Discovery Readiness—Pre-School	A complete program of learning experiences designed to build readiness skills in all subject areas.
Xerox Education Center	Personalized Reading Center 4, 5, 6	This center offers books to children of every ability in a self-instructional program.

APPENDIX E

Games

Bremer—Davis Phonics
The Sound Way to Easy Reading

Childcraft Equipment
  Kiddiecraft's 300 Common Words
  Teaching Typewriter
Creative Playthings
  Reading Lotto (Zoo, City, House)
Curriculum Associates
  Vocabulary Builder Series
    Syllabo
    Phantonyms
    Synonimbies
Educational Games, Inc.
  Wonder Words
Ed-U-Cards Corporation
  Schoolhouse in a Fun Box
The Garrard Press
  Dolch Aids-To-Reading Materials
  Picture Readiness Game
  Who Gets It?
  Match, Set 1
  Match, Set 2
  Consonant Cards
  Vowel Cards
  Picture Word Cards
  Popper Words, Set 1 (Group Size)
  Popper Words, Set 1
  Popper Words, Set 2
  Basic Sight Cards
  Sight Phrase Cards
  What the Letters Says
  Consonant Lotto
  Vowel Lotto
  Take
  Syllable Game
  Group Sounding Game
  Read and Say Verb Game
Harper and Row, Inc.
  Word-Go-Round
Houghton Mifflin
  Getset Games
    Set of 8 games

Ideal School Supply Company
  Quiet Pal Game
  The End-in-E Game
  Rhyming Puzzle
  Magic Card Opposites
  Magic Cards Consonant Blends
  Magic Cards Initial Consonants
  Magic Cards Vowels
Instructo Company
  Instructo
      Fun with Rhymes Activity Kit
Johnson Library of Reading Aids
  Shuffle 'N Read
Kenworthy Educational Service, Inc.
  Phonic Rummy
Lyons and Carnahan, Inc.
  Phonics We Use—Learning Games Kit
Milton Bradley
  Dial 'N Spell
  Goal: Language Development—337 Game Kit
  Password
Montessori Educational Games
  Ends 'N Blends
F. A. Owen Publishing Company
  Picto-Word Flash Cards
Selchow & Righter Co.
  Scrabble
  Scrabble for Juniors
3M Brand EduPLAYtional Games
  Teach Key (Reading & Spelling)

Audio-Visual Devices

Bell and Howell
Language Master
  Students may compare their own pronunciation of words to the manufacturer's or teacher's correct pronunciations with this machine and the series of special sound cards.

Educational Activities, Inc.

"U" Filmstrip Kit

This handy kit, ideal for original projects, contains 25 feet of 35mm film that can be typewritten on or marked with pen or pencil. It also contains a spray-on coating and a quick splicer plus storage cans and felt tip pens.

EDL/McGraw-Hill

EDL Aud-X

This is an audio-visual teaching machine that uses both film-strip cassettes and tape cassettes. Table-top projection screens and headsets are available. A variety of materials such as story kits and word study kits are available on all levels for use with the Aud-X.

EDL Controlled Reader

The controlled reader presents projected material at a controlled rate in a left to right, line by line manner.

EDL Controlled Reader, Jr.

This reader is smaller and is designed for individual or small group use.

EDL Skimmer

The skimmer is mainly a rate motivator and timing monitor which helps the able reader to increase his reading rate. A beam of light is projected down the centerfold of a page at a rate of 30 seconds per page. Skimming and Scanning Texts and Work-books should be ordered separately for use with this machine.

EDL Flash-X Tachistoscope

The Flash-X is a round, hand-sized device with a flasher set at $\frac{1}{25}$ of a second. Special discs are available to provide practice in visual perception and word attack skills.

EDL Tach-X Tachistoscope

The tachistoscope presents material in timed exposures for the purpose of developing visual discrimination, visual memory and sight vocabulary.

Educational Projections Corporation

Standard 888 Programmed Filmstrip Viewer

This filmstrip projector has four response buttons which the student presses to answer the filmstrip's multiple choice questions. If the answer is correct, a green light will flash and a buzzer will sound. A wide variety of tapes are available on the elementary level for use with this machine.

ERCA
Tutorgram

Students can work individually on various skills with this handy individual unit. The student selects responses by inserting the attached pointer into a circle by his selected response. A buzzer will sound for the correct answer. A variety of cards are available for use with the Tutorgram.

Singer/Graflex Division
Auto-Vance II Study Mate

Filmstrips and sound cassettes can be combined for use in this compact automatic unit designed for individual or small group viewing.

E-Z Viewer

This small, convenient device for filmstrip viewing is designed for individual use and can even be held in the hand.

Messenger VII

This is an automatic advance cassette/filmstrip projector with a 8-¾" x 6-¼" screen. Phone speaker jacks are available for individual listening.

Study Mate II

This is a sturdy 35mm rear screen filmstrip projector ideal for individual use.

AV Media

Americana Interstate Corporation
Listen and Learn with Phonics

This kit contains books and records dealing with the phonic approach to pronouncing unknown words.

Associated Press
Reading Kit

This kit for developing auditory and sight discrimination contains records, letter cards, lotto games, a board game and many suggestions for further activities.

EDL/McGraw Hill
Listen and Read

This program is designed to increase listening and reading skills on the seventh grade to adult level. The instructional materials include thirty tapes and a companion workbook on each level.

Listen and Think

This program includes fifteen tapes and a lesson book on each level from K-9. These tapes provide systematic and sequential instruction in analytical, interpretive, appreciative and critical listening and thinking skills.

Educational Record Sales
Sounds for Young Readers

Phonetic principles teaching auditory discrimination, consonants and vowels are included in this material for the primary student.

Eye Gate House, Inc.
Advanced Reading Skills

This wide range program covers topics relating to literature and famous places, the origin and meaning of words, the selection of words, the association of facts and ideas and creative talent.

Adventures in Reading

In this filmstrip library, a variety of good books are summarized.

Enjoying Poetry

Several well known poems are depicted on this collection of filmstrips.

Fundamentals of Language Arts

Included in this program are materials covering such skills as critical thinking, problem solving, interpreting, summarizing, observing and analyzing.

Fundamentals of Vocabulary Building

This program includes materials which explore the vocabulary skills dealing with prefixes and suffixes, the singular and plural forms of words, homonyms, synonyms and the use of the dictionary and other reference books.

Ideal
Listen-Look-Learn Reading Tapes and Cassettes
This is a complete library of tapes or cassettes dealing with a wide range of word attack skills.

Imperial Productions, Inc.
Imperial Instructional Tapes
Comprehension and word attack skills are presented in a self-teaching program consisting of 40 tapes. The tapes are designed for primary children.

International Teaching Tapes, Inc.
Reading Improvement Series—Primary
Reading Improvement Series—Intermediate
Each program consists of forty audio tapes which present basic word attack and comprehension skills through a variety of interesting and informative stories, articles, songs and rhymes.

McGraw-Hill
Learning Language Skills: A Creative Approach 1, 2, 3, 4.
A wide variety of media is used to encourage beginning language development. This program meets both group and individual needs for ages four through eight.

McGraw-Hill
+10 Vocabulary Booster
This is a radio and/or cassette program of systematic vocabulary development for use in the middle grades. It is intended to increase knowledge of word meanings in the content areas.

Charles E. Merrill Publishing Company
Reading and Phonics Skilltapes
This program contains tapes on multi-levels in reading and phonic skill abilities. These tapes are designed to accompany the Merrill Skilltexts or to be used as teacher aids in an individualized instructional program.
Spoken Arts Cassette Libraries
Complete Library for Young Listeners Vol. I (50 cassettes)

Complete Library for Young Listeners Vol. II (50 cassettes)
Complete Library for Intermediate Listeners (50 cassettes)
Complete Library for Advanced Listeners (50 cassettes)
Mini-Libraries (6 cassettes)

This library of varied works is designed to cultivate literary appreciation, imagination, listening skills and develop memory.

New Dimensions in Education
Alpha Time

This multi-media pre-reading program features the "Huggables" which are inflated letter people. The entire readiness program is built around these delightful, alliterative characters such as Mr. M—Munchy Mouth or Mr. T—Tall Teeth.
Alpha One

A beginning reading program with a wide variety of colorful components such as hard cover readers, puppets, story pictures and filmstrips all featuring the "Letter People."

Random House School Division
Aware: A Poetry Learning Unit

This unique and interesting poetry kit contains activity cards, track cards, poetry booklets, tape cassettes and scent samples.

Singer
Slides

This collection of 2″ x 2″ color slides stimulates imagination and vocabulary development in students of all ages by providing a starting point for expression.

Society for Visual Education
Basic Primary Phonics and Filmstrips Series

This is a collection of seventeen filmstrips presenting information on basic phonic skills. It can be used in grades one to three.

Taylor Associates
"Tell Me a Story"

"Tell Me a Story" is a collection of fine children's literature presented on filmstrip and record or cassette. Tell-Back books and the regular book are included in the library. Presently there are nine libraries with each containing four stories.

Teacher Resources

Acoustifone Corporation
Kids' Stuff—Kindergarten and Nursery School
Kids' Stuff, Reading and Spelling—Primary

Fearon Publishers
Creative Activities for the Gifted Child
   This is a collection of over 100 classroom tested ideas for independent work.

Ginn and Company

V Is for Verse	Teacher
Let's Listen	Primary
Let's Play a Game	Primary
Reading Activities for Middle Grades	Intermediate
Help Yourself to Read, Write and Spell	Intermediate

The Garrard Press
Games and Stunts to Read and Play, Set 1, Book 1 (Primary)
Read and Play, Set 1, Books 2 and 3 (Primary)
Read and Play, Set 2, Books 1, 2 and 3 (Primary)
Spache, Evelyn B.: *Reading Activities for Child Involvement.* Boston, Allyn and Bacon, Inc., 1972.
   Fun and helpful activities to aid in the teaching of reading are found in this book.

University of Missouri at Kansas City and Calvin Productions: "A Walk Away in the Rain." New York, Holt, Rinehart, and Winston, 1968.
   The problems involved in motivating a bright student are examined in this open-end film.

APPENDIX F

List of Publishers and Their Addresses

   This list contains the addresses of publishing companies mentioned in this book.
ACOUSTIFONE CORPORATION, 20149 Sunburst Street, Chatsworth, Calif. 91311.

ALLYN AND BACON, INC., Rockleigh, N. J. 07647.

AMERICAN BOOK COMPANY, 450 West 33rd Street, New York, N. Y. 10001.

AMERICAN EDUCATION PUBLICATIONS, Xerox Education Group, 245 Long Hill Rd., Middletown, Conn. 06457.

AMERICAN GEOGRAPHICAL SOCIETY, Broadway at 156 Street, New York, N. Y. 10032.

AMERICAN HERITAGE PUBLISHING COMPANY, 379 W. Clinton Street, Marion, Ohio 43302.

AMERICAN LIBRARY ASSOCIATION, 50 East Huron Street, Chicago, Ill. 60611.

AMERICAN MUSEUM OF NATURAL HISTORY, Central Park West at 79th Street, New York, N. Y. 10024.

AMERICAN NATIONAL RED CROSS, 18th & D Street, N. W., Washington, D. C. 20006.

AMERICAN POLITICAL SCIENCE ASSOCIATION, 3937 Chestnut Street, Philadelphia, Pa. 19104.

AMERICANA INTERSTATE CORPORATION, Mundelein, Ill. 60060.

ANTIOCH PRESS, P.O. Box 148, Yellow Springs, Ohio 45387

APPLETON-CENTURY-CROFTS, INC., Division of Meredith Publishing Company, 440 Park Avenue, S., New York, N.Y. 10016.

ASSOCIATED PRESS, P.O. Box 5, Teaneck, N. J. 07666.

ATLANTIC MONTHLY, 125 Garden Street, Marion, Ohio 43302.

ATLAS: BEST FROM THE WORLD PRESS, Subscription Dept., Box 2550, Boulder, Colo. 80302.

BALDRIDGE READING INSTRUCTION MATERIALS, INC., Fourteen Grigg Street, Greenwich, Conn. 06830.

BARNELL LOFT, LTD., 111 South Centre Avenue, Rockville Centre, New York, N. Y. 11571.

BELL & HOWELL COMPANY, Audio-Visual Products Division, 7100 McCormack Blvd., Chicago, Ill. 60645.

BENEFIC PRESS, 10300 West Roosevelt Road, Westchester, Ill. 60153.

BOBBS-MERRILL COMPANY, INC., 4300 W. 62 Street, Indianapolis, Ind. 46268.

BOOKPLAN, 46 Jane Street, New York, N.Y. 10014.

BOWMAR, 622 Rodier Drive, Glendale, Calif. 91201.

BOY SCOUTS OF AMERICA, North Brunswick, N. J. 08902.

BREMER-DAVIS PHONICS, 161 Green Bay Road, Wilmette, Ill. 60091.

WILLIAM C. BROWN BOOK COMPANY, 135 Locust Street, Dubuque, Iowa 52001.

CALIFORNIA STATE DEPT. OF EDUCATION, Sacramento, Calif.

CHILDCRAFT EQUIPMENT, 964 Third Avenue, New York, N. Y. 10022.

CHILDREN'S BOOK CENTER, University of Chicago, Graduate Library School, Chicago, Ill. 60637.

CHILDREN'S BOOK COUNCIL, 175 Fifth Avenue, New York, N. Y. 10010.

THE CHRISTOPHER PUBLISHING HOUSE, 53 Billings Rd., N. Quincy, Mass. 02171.

CONGRESSIONAL DIGEST CORPORATION, 3231 P Street, N. W., Washington, D. C. 20007.

CONGRESSIONAL QUARTERLY, INC., 1735 K Street, N. W., Washington, D. C. 20006.

CREATIVE PLAYTHINGS, Princeton, N. J. 08540.

CRISIS: A RECORD OF THE DARK RACES, 1790 Broadway, New York, N. Y. 10019.

CURRICULUM ASSOCIATES, P.O. Box 56, Wellesley, Mass. 02181.

DELL PUBLISHING COMPANY, 750 Third Avenue, New York, N. Y. 10017.

NELSON DOUBLEDAY, INC., Garden City, N. Y. 11531.

E. P. DUTTON AND COMPANY, INC., 201 Park Avenue S., New York, N. Y. 10003.

E & R DEVELOPMENT COMPANY, INC., Subsidiary of Hertzberg-New Method, Inc., Candalia Rd., Jacksonville, Ill. 62650.

ED-U-CARDS CORPORATION, Commack, N. Y. 11725.

EDUCATIONAL ACTIVITIES, INC., P.O. Box 392, Freeport, N. Y. 11520.

EDUCATIONAL DEVELOPMENT LABORATORIES, INC.,

Division of McGraw-Hill, 284 Pulaski Rd., Huntington, N. Y. 11744.

EDUCATIONAL GAMES, INC., P.O. Box 5833, Grand Central Station, New York, N. Y. 10017.

EDUCATIONAL PROJECTIONS CORPORATION, 1911 Pickwick, Avenue, Glenview, Ill. 60025.

EDUCATIONAL RECORD SALES, 153 Chambers Street, New York, N. Y. 10007.

EDUCATORS PUBLISHING SERVICE, 301 Vassar Street, Cambridge, Mass. 02139.

ELECTRONIC FUTURES, INC., 57 Dodge Avenue, North Haven, Conn. 06473.

ENVIRONMENTAL ACTION, INC., Room 731, 1346 Connecticut Avenue N. W., Washington, D. C. 20036.

ENRICHMENT READING CORPORATION OF AMERICA, Iron Ridge, Wis. 53035.

EYE GATE HOUSE, INC., 146–01 Archer Avenue, Jamaica, N. Y. 11435.

FEARON PUBLISHER, INC., 6 Davis Drive, Belmont, Calif. 94002.

FIELD EDUCATIONAL PUBLICATIONS, INC., 2400 Hanover Street, Palo Alto, Calif. 94304.

FOLLETT EDUCATIONAL CORPORATION, P.O. Box 5705, Chicago, Ill. 60680.

THE GARRARD PRESS, 510 North Hickory Street, Champaign, Ill. 61820.

GINN COMPANY, 125 Second Avenue, Waltham, Mass. 02154.

GIRL SCOUTS OF THE USA, 830 Third Avenue, New York, N. Y. 10022.

GROLIER READING PROGRAM, INC., Sherman Turnpike, Danbury, Conn. 06810.

C. S. HAMMOND, INC., 515 Valley Street, Maplewood, N. J. 07040.

HARCOURT, BRACE & JOVANOVICH, 757 3rd Avenue, New York, N. Y. 10017.

HARPER & ROW PUBLISHERS, 49 East 33rd Street, New York, N. Y. 10016.

IRVIN HASS, Book Club Consultants, 65 Diana's Trail, Roslyn Estates, N. Y. 11576.

D. C. HEATH AND COMPANY, 285 Columbus Avenue, Boston, Mass. 02116.

HIGHLIGHTS FOR CHILDREN, 2300 West 5th Avenue, Columbus, Ohio 43216.

HOFFMAN INFORMATION SYSTEMS, INC., 2626 South Peck Road, Monrovia, Calif. 91016.

HOLT, RINEHART AND WINSTON, 383 Madison Avenue, New York, N. Y. 10017.

HOUGHTON-MIFFLIN COMPANY, Educational Division, 110 Tremont Street, Boston, Mass. 02107.

IDEAL SCHOOL SUPPLY COMPANY, 8312–8346 Birkhoff Avenue, Chicago, Ill. 60620.

IMPERIAL PRODUCTIONS, INC., 247 West Court Street, Kankakee, Ill. 60901.

INTERNATIONAL READING ASSOCIATION, 6 Tyre Avenue, Newark, Del. 19711.

INTERNATIONAL TEACHING TAPES, INC., A Subsidiary of Educational Development Corporation, Palo Alto, Calif. 94306.

INERNATIONAL TEXTBOOK, Division of Intext Educational Publishers, Oak Street & Pawnee Avenue, Scranton, Penn. 18515.

INSTRUCTO COMPANY, Paoli, Penn. 19301.

INTERSTATE PRINTERS AND PUBLISHERS, 19–27 N. Jackson Street, Danville, Ill., 61832.

JOHNSON LIBRARY OF READING AIDS, Box 68, Rochelle, Ill. 61068.

JOHNSON PUBLISHING COMPANY, 1820 S. Michigan Avenue, Chicago, Ill. 60611.

JUNIOR DISCOVERERS BOOK CLUB, 154 E. Erie Street, Chicago, Ill. 60611.

JUNIOR LITERARY GUILD, Division of Doubleday & Company, 277 Park Avenue, New York, N. Y. 10017.

KENWORTHY EDUCATIONAL SERVICE, INC., P.O. Box 3031, Buffalo, N. Y. 14205.

KIDS, P.O. Box 3041, Grand Central Station, New York, N. Y. 10017.

LEARN, INC., 21 East Euclid Avenue, Haddonfield, N. J. 08033.

LYONS & CARNAHAN, INC., 407 East 25 Street, Chicago, Ill. 60616.

McCORMICK MATHERS, 300 Pike Street, Cincinnati, Ohio 45202.

McGRAW-HILL BOOK COMPANY, 330 West 42nd Street, New York, N. Y. 10036.

DAVID McKAY COMPANY, INC., 750 Third Avenue, New York, N. Y. 10017.

THE MACMILLAN COMPANY, 434 South Wabash Avenue, Chicago, Ill. 60605.

MAFEX ASSOCIATES, Box 519, Johnston, Penn. 15907.

CHARLES E. MERRILL BOOKS, INC., 1300 Alum Creek Drive, Columbus, Ohio 43216.

MILTON BRADLEY COMPANY, 74 Park Street, Springfield, Mass. 01105.

MONTESSORI EDUCATIONAL GAMES, Division of Dac Toymakers, Inc., Farmingdale, N. Y. 11735.

MSS EDUCATIONAL PUBLISHING COMPANY, INC., 655 Madison Avenue, New York, N. Y. 10021.

NATION ASSOCIATES, INC., 333 Sixth Avenue, New York, N. Y. 10014.

NATIONAL AUDUBON SOCIETY, 1130 Fifth Avenue, New York, N. Y. 10028.

NATIONAL GEOGRAPHIC SOCIETY, 17th & M Streets, N. W., Washington, D. C. 20036.

NATIONAL OBSERVER, 200 Barnett Road, Chicopee, Mass. 01021.

NATIONAL WILDLIFE FEDERATION, 1412 Sixteenth Street, N. W., Washington, D. C. 20036.

NEW DIMENSIONS IN EDUCATION, INC., 160 DuPont Street, Plainview, N. Y. 18803.

NEW YORK ZOOLOGICAL SOCIETY, 185 St. & Southern Blvd., New York, N. Y. 10460.

NEWSWEEK SUBSCRIPTION SERVICE, Newsweek Building, Livingston, N. J. 07039.

NOBLE & NOBLE, 750 Third Avenue, New York, N. Y. 10017.

ODYSSEY PRESS (Bobbs, Merrill), 4300 W. 62 Street, Indianapolis, Ind. 46268.

F. A. OWEN PUBLISHING COMPANY, Dansville, N. Y. 14437.

PARENT'S MAGAZINE ENTERPRISES, INC., 52 Vanderbilt Avenue, New York, N. Y. 10017.

PARKER PUBLISHING COMPANY, INC., West Nyack, N. Y. 10994.

PERMA BOUND (Hertzberg-New Method), Vandalia Road, Jacksonvile, Ill. 62650.

SIR ISAAC PITMAN AND SON, LTD., Pitman House, 39 Parker Street, London, England.

PLAYS, INC., 8 Arlington Street, Boston, Mass. 02116.

PRENTICE-HALL, INC., Englewood Cliffs, N. J. 07632.

PYRAMID BOOKS, 9 Garden Street, Moonachie, N. J. 07074.

RANDOM HOUSE, 457 Madison Avenue, New York, N. Y. 10022.

READERS AND WRITERS, 130–21 224 Street, Jamaica, N. Y. 11413.

READER'S DIGEST EDUCATIONAL DIVISION, Pleasantville, N. Y. 10570.

REVIEW PUBLISHNG COMPANY, 1100 Waterway Blvd., Indianapolis, Ind. 46202.

SATURDAY EVENING POST COMPANY, 1100 Waterways Blvd., Indianapolis, Ind. 46202.

SATURDAY REVIEW, INC., 380 Madison Avenue, New York, N. Y. 10017.

THE SCARECROW PRESS, INC., Subsidiary of Grolier, Inc., 52 Liberty Street, Box 656, Metuchen, N. J. 08840.

SCHOLASTIC BOOK SERVICES, 50 West 44th Street, New York, N. Y. 10036.

SCIENCE RESEARCH ASSOCIATES, INC., 165 University Avenue, Palo Alto, Calif. 94301.

SCOTT FORESMAN & COMPANY, 1900 E. Lake Avenue, Glenview, Ill. 60025.

SELCHOW & RIGHTER, 200 5th Avenue, New York, N. Y. 10020.

SESAME STREET MAGAZINE, North Road, Poughkeepsie, N. Y. 12201.

SEVENTEEN SUBSCRIPTION DEPARTMENT, Triangle Communications, Inc., Radnor, Penn. 19088.

SIMON AND SCHUSTER, INC., Rockefeller Center, 630 Fifth Avenue, New York, N. Y. 10020.

THE SINGER COMPANY, Graflex Division, Rochester, N. Y. 14603.

SOCIETY FOR VISUAL EDUCATION, 1345 Diversey Parkway, Chicago, Ill. 60614.

SOCIETY OF THE SIGMA XI, 155 Whitney Avenue, New Haven, Conn. 16510.

TAYLOR ASSOCIATES, Hawk Drive, Lloyd Harbor, N. Y. 11743.

TEACHERS COLLEGE PRESS, Columbia University, 525 West 120th Street, New York, N. Y. 10027.

CHARLES C THOMAS PUBLISHER, 301–327 East Lawrence Avenue, Springfield, Ill. 62717.

3M BRAND EDUPLAYTIONAL GAMES, 3M Center, St. Paul, Minn. 55101.

TIME, INC., 541 N. Fairbanks, Ct., Chicago, Ill. 60611.

TRAVEL MAGAZINE, INC., Travel Bldg., Floral Park, N. Y. 11001.

TRIDENT PRESS, Division of Simon & Shuster, Inc., 630 5th Avenue, New York, N. Y. 10020.

UNITED CHAPTERS OF PHI BETA KAPPA, 1811 Q Street, N. W., Washington, D. C. 20009.

U. S. NEWS & WORLD REPORT, Circulation Department, 435 Parker Avenue, Dayton, Ohio 45401.

UNIVERSITY OF MINNESOTA PRESS, 2037 University Ave., S. E., Minneapolis, Minn. 55455.

WESTERN PUBLISHING COMPANY, INC., 1220 Mound Avenue, Racine, Wis. 53404.

WISCONSIN BOOK CLUB, INC., Box 223, Grafton, Wis. 53024.

XEROX EDUCATIONAL CENTER, Columbus, Ohio 43216.

YOUNG READERS PRESS, INC., Subsidiary of Charter Communications, Inc., 1120 Avenue of the Americas, New York, N. Y. 10036.

AUTHOR INDEX

SUBJECT INDEX